Patrik Schlesinger

The process of creating everything you want

YOU ARE

the

SUCCESS

DESIGN YOUR LIFE YOU LIVE
AND BE WHERE YOU WANT TO BE
WITH ALL
THE GREATEST POSSIBILITIES
WHICH ARE STILL
IN YOU

Take the most successful journey right now

"Peace, Silence and Harmony."

"I would like to tell you a story about
The Biggest Secret.
The Biggest Secret is, that there is no secret at all.
There was only many and many definitions to catch
you in the never ending information values of
ignorance.
Just be Patient, Persistent and in Harmony
with your own Reality,
because you are already a successful Human Being."

Patrik Schlesinger

CONTENT

"How to use this book to help you get everything you want."

𝔘nderstanding of a fundamental experience in life, you

bring your personal truth to every act you do in every moment. Each of us has his own life story and my life story can be described by a Poem written by *Idries Shah ("Story of Fatima – The Spinner and the tent")*. I invite you to read this beautiful life story of Fatima right here and right now:

> *"Once in a city in the Farthest West there lived a girl called Fatima. She was the daughter of a prosperous spinner. One day her father said to her: "Come, daughter, we are going on a journey, for I have business in the islands of the Middle Sea. Perhaps you may find some handsome youth in a good situation whom you could take as husband. "*

> *They set off and travelled from island to island, the father doing his trading while Fatima dreamt of the husband who might soon be hers. One day, however, they were on the way to Crete when a storm blew up and the ship was wrecked. Fatima, only half-conscious, was cast up on the seashore near Alexandria.*

> *Her father was dead and she was utterly destitute. She could only remember dimly her life until then, for her experience of the shipwreck and her exposure in the sea, had utterly exhausted her.*

While she was wandering on the sands, a family of cloth-makers found her. Although they were poor, they took her into their humble home and taught her their craft. Thus it was that she made a second life for herself and within a year or two she was happy and reconciled to her lot.

But one day, when she was on the seashore for some reason, a band of slave-traders landed and carried her, along with other captives, away with them. Although she bitterly lamented her lot, Fatima found no sympathy from the slavers, who took her to Istanbul and sold her as a slave. Her world had collapsed for the second time.

Now it chanced that there were few buyers at the market. One of them was a man who was looking for slaves to work in his wood yard, where he made masts for ships. When he saw the dejection of the unfortunate Fatima, he decided to buy her, thinking that in this way, at least, he might be able to give her a slightly better life than if she were bought by someone else.

He took Fatima to his home, intending to make her a serving-maid for his wife. When he arrived at the house, however, he found that he had lost all his money in a cargo which had been captured by pirates. He could not afford workers, so he, Fatima and his wife were left alone to work at the heavy labor of making masts. Fatima, grateful to her employer for rescuing her, worked so hard and so well that he gave her freedom and she became his trusted helper. Thus it was that she became comparatively happy in her third career.

One day he said to her: "Fatima, I want you to go with a cargo of ships' masts to Java, as my agent and be sure that you will turn a profit." She set off, but when the ship was off the coast of China a typhoon wrecked it and Fatima found herself again cast up on the seashore of a strange land.

Once again she wept bitterly, for she felt that nothing in her life was working in accordance with expectation. Whenever things seemed to be going well, something came and destroyed all her hopes. "Why is it", she cried out, for the third time, "that whenever I try to do something it comes to grief? Why should so many unfortunate things happen to me?" But there was no answer.

So she picked herself up from the sand and started to walk inland. Now it so happened that nobody in China had heard of Fatima, or knew anything about her troubles. But there was a legend that a certain stranger, a woman, would one day arrive there and that she would be able to make a tent for the Emperor. And since there was as yet nobody in China who could make tents, everyone looked upon the fulfilment of this prediction with the liveliest anticipation. In order to make sure that this stranger, when she arrived, would not be missed, successive Emperors of China had followed the custom of sending heralds, once a year, to all the towns and villages of the land, asking for any foreign woman to be produced at Court.

When Fatima stumbled into a town by the Chinese seashore, it was one such occasion. The people spoke to her through an interpreter and explained that she would have to go to see the Emperor. "Lady," said the Emperor, when Fatima was brought before him, "can you make a tent?" "I think so," said Fatima. She asked for rope, but there was none to be had. So, remembering her time as a spinner, she collected flax and made ropes. Then she asked for stout cloth, but the Chinese had none of the kind which she needed. So, drawing on her experience with the weavers of Alexandria, she made some stout tent cloth. Then she found that she needed tent-poles, but there were none in China. So Fatima, remembering how she had been trained by the wood-fashioner of Istanbul, cunningly made stout tent-poles.

When these were ready, she racked her brains for the memory of all the tents she had seen in her travels: and lo, a tent was made. When this wonder was revealed to the Emperor of China, he offered Fatima the fulfillment of any wish she cared to name. She chose to settle in China, where she married a handsome prince and where she remained in happiness, surrounded by her children, until the end of her days.

It was through these adventures that Fatima realized that what had appeared to be an unpleasant experience at the time, turned out to be an essential part of the making of her ultimate happiness."

What's in this Initiation Poem for me? Great Blessing to be helpful for myself and others. All this beautiful Blessing of Knowledge I'm giving you as a big THANK YOU in this book.

What's next for you? All the information values provided in this book, I teach my friends and clients for their personal needs to be successful, so take all of it, transform it within you and use it in your way for all your actual needs.

This book is divided into systematic and strategic sections that show you many possibilities how to get from where you are to where you want to be. Of course, it carries a great deal of personal responsibility. Therefore, first read the entire book and based on the information values that are close to you, decide whether you want to include the described practices in your miraculous life expression.

Your success is everywhere and takeable every time you want, your success is searching you, your success is straight here, where you are now. The Success is YOU.

Take the most successful journey right now and achieve an extraordinary results you deserve!

Patrik Schlesinger

Chapter one

"Success is beyond time, space and causation"

COMMUNICATION FOR SUCCESS

Amazed I have to say, yes, success is beyond time, space and causation. Success is limitless and have no name. Success in something, that is unmanifested, which is beyond thought, word, act, beyond all of that which has form, weight, beyond everything you know.

What a success means to you cannot be a guaranteed success for someone else and so on the contrary. Each of us has its own definition of success, but success in its unmanifested state is just something that can be felt. It gains its specificity through dual thinking, thus accepting a lack of something around you associated with observed of your five senses. Thus, only a tangible success of others which you observe with the five senses, can be given a specific name. In this way, it acquires its concrete specificity and personal importance.

How to get from where you are to where you want to be?
This is the most frequent question that I heard from my clients and friends. To understand that, you have to go beyond time, space and causation and to know the rules of communication. To know the rules of communication, you have to know, what the communication is.

SCHEME OF COMMUNICATION

everything is manifestation of your thoughts

UNMANIFESTED
TRUE COMMUNICATION

DESTRUCTIVE	CONSTRUCTIVE
SOCIAL COMMUNICATION	CONSCIOUS COMMUNICATION
THOUGHT - WORD - ACTION	THOUGHT - WORD - ACTION

MANIFESTED
THOUGHT - WORD - ACTION
IN THE DUALITY

Unmanifested Communication

Unmanifested Communication is the place, where your successful journey begins and where it returns. Here is all your limitlessness. It is the Absolute Indescribable Freedom to achieve everything you ask for. This is the place where you are and where you want to be. This is the place, from which you every day acted unconsciously, but with this moment you act Absolutely Consciously.

In the place of Unmanifested Communication you find all the so called "feelings and powers", that you could not describe, but they was every time so powerful. You knew about them, but you did not know what to do with them. *"What a great feeling is it, what should I do with it?"*, *"I know, that there is something, but I cannot describe it, but it is there, I feel It."*, *"What a beautiful vibrating energy is around me."*, or *"What a power."* etc. All this and many more felt facts are what I call here as Unmanifested Communication and this is one possible explaining of one very old, bud Absolutely True quotation: *"What you are searching for, is searching you."* We can explain it also schematically:

$$\frac{WHAT}{SEARCHING} = \textit{Unmanifested Communication}$$

or also

The word WHAT + the word SEARCHING = *Unmanifested Communication*

or also

The *WHAT* **IS** *SEARCHING* **YOU**

This indescribable "feelings and powers" are the motor for whole creating and I got some keys for you to manifest something concrete from this place of Truth.

You heard from many trainers, coaches, consultants, motivational speakers, etc., that *"nothing comes from nothing"* and that you have to take an action. I say: *"Everything comes every time from indescribable nothing without any acting."* This is exactly that, what I see daily in my practice. The people still become everything, what they want and they don't know, from where it is coming to them.

In order to understand the above written, first of all, you have to know what communication of creating really is and what rules / laws it have. It is very important to understand this principles, to admit this principles, to act with this principles and to give the principles further.

Unmanifested Communication is beyond time, space and causation, so let's go to handle it.

BEYOND TIME – The concept of time is the most misunderstood and most discussed phenomenon of our whole human race. We saw thousands and thousands of complicated theories and speculations, which did not bring any benefit. Yet, it is very simple and easy to understand.

"Free your mind from the concept of time, space and causation and you opened the door to the source of creation."

It is said, that time is life. I say, Time is life's survival, not life itself. Therefore, whoever doesn't depend on concept of time, controls his real life.

Remember the times when you were a child. At that time, you do not deal with the concept of time. You just did what you wanted and how simple it was. You have to recreate this simple thinking right now in this moment.

Following practice you can easily and comfortable practice every day. I just recommend you simplicity in every aspect of your daily life expression.

Practice

From this moment, three times a day, think about that, that there is no time. In this moment you think like this, just stop doing things for a while, breathe slowly and feel the passion of a current moment.

At the end of this practice, you can do what you have to do with words: *"Here I am, in the present moment, let's go further."* Of course, use every time your own words. The results, or fruits of this practice, will come very quickly over the next few days. You'll be amazed to see what you have unconsciously overlooked.

Understanding the concept of time is your most precious resource how to be successful in every moment of your life. For this you have to know, that feelings and powers are the most valuable thing you actually have. Feelings and powers are indicators of your abilities and the difference between success and failure. Feelings and powers are something that you still use to increase productivity. Feelings and powers are the essential upon which everything else in life depends. Feelings and powers are dancers in the rhythm of creating. Feelings and powers are before all desires. Yes, they are! Did you know that the desires with willpower are bigger than the mind itself? Think for a moment. When the desires and willpower are bigger than the mind itself, how big are the feelings and powers behind them? How big potential is in you?

Do you see the indescribable, beautiful and powerful potential which dwells in you? Do you feel it now? Just take it and transform it for whatever you like.

The very act of taking a moment to stop act and think, is beginning to transform your personal time management and increase productivity immediately.

The real time management have no time, they have only peace of possibilities of current moment. That is essential to know, because actually presented time management in the world is only a business tool, which steal you your personal inner feelings and powers (your whole personality). Never be a slave of time, never be a slave of thousands of theories and never be a slave of someone else. Just be yourself in every moment.

Now you see, that beyond time there are all the greatest feelings and powers, which are before every thought, word and act! Now you see the importance of peace and silence. If you touch the dimension beyond time, everything is becoming as the title now. Concept of time is extremely relative and is only one of many other mediators between the unconsciousness and consciousness.

BEYOND SPACE – The concept of space is the second most misunderstood and second most discussed phenomenon of our whole human race. Here we see as by the "time theories" also a lot of complicated theories and speculations, which did not bring any benefit. Yet, it is also very simple and easy to understand.

"Free your mind from the concept of time, space and causation and you are opened the door to the source of creation."

The whole perception of the space has degenerated into perceptions of five senses. I consider this as a tragedy of ignorance. The real space of creating is beyond that space we perceive with our five senses. That's the place, where the unmanifested communication occur. That's the real place, where you build your five sense space – the whole world around you. That's the place, where your feelings and powers are transformed in something concrete and from where is manifested everything you want. That's the point, why you can say: "If I can see it Inside, I can hold it outside." If you choose the feeling and power of being in this space and you just stay in it for a while, it become as sensible as anything else you already know. This is how you create from inside. You can get better than before, just take more care of your inner system of creation. Maybe you cared too much to satisfy someone else. Maybe you spent your time trying to become like someone else. In other words, in finding harmony with others, you can never find the gratification you are looking for. Therefore, first of all you have to be in harmony with yourself. Free yourself from all the thoughts of tension that has departed you from who you really are and go only in that direction that you want. You should also know, that if you did not taste what you did not want, you would not come to what you really want. Everything you do is absolutely fine. You have to accept that you are free and valuable not only for this world, but for whole Universe. Yes, you are. You see how it works and how simple and easy is it? You are the creator of your own space.

Following practice you can easily and comfortable practice at every place and every day. I just recommend you simplicity in every aspect of your daily life expression.

Practice

From this moment, three times a day, think about that, that there is no space. In this moment you think like this, just stop doing things for a while, breathe slowly and feel the passion of a current moment. Now say (it is not important to express these words or not): "There is something important here. What is that, what I want right now?"

At the end of this practice, you can do what you have to do with those words: *"Here I am, at this place, let's go further."* Of course, use it every time with your own words. The results or fruits of this practice, will come very quickly over the next few days. You'll be amazed to see also with this practice, what you have unconsciously overlooked.

Great to know, that you can use your space how you like. It's only your space, so take all yours knowing to transform it. You and the space are one, there is no difference, because you created it and you are the creator of it, through described inner feelings and powers. Therefore, always act according to your feelings and not according to your thoughts, because act through thoughts caused only lack and pain.

BEYOND CAUSATION – The concept of causation is the third most misunderstood and third most discussed phenomenon of our whole human race. Here we see, as by time and space theories, also a lot of complicated theories and speculations, which did not bring any benefit. Yet, it also is very simple and easy to understand.

"Free your mind from the concept of time, space and causation and you are opened the door to the source of creation."

As you can see, there is something behind your five senses. This fact becomes simple and easy for you to see when you analyze how your daily life expression functions. You see also, that you can only know that through your own experience. Your personal experience is not transferable, it can only be further provided.

Look at life expression as it is. What you can see? Everything what you can observe with your senses is in constant change. Nothing is motionless. This is standard explanation of physics. But how is it possible? There are many and many phenomenon every day, which are beyond the physical and other laws. They are beyond your perception. This is because consciousness was sleeping.

Consciousness is beyond causation, beyond cause and effect. Cause and effect occurs only by one accepting the laws of social system. That's it. Nothing more, nothing less. That acceptance means to be in borders or limitations of someone else.

Consciousness is beyond physical form, beyond senses, beyond cognition and beyond mental state. That means, to be conscious, you have to be free from everything you've ever known. You have to thrust only yourself.

The modern way of thinking assumes that everything that you can observe has its own cause. In one hand, cause and effect is the law that balances everything manifested and consciousness is beyond them.

Following practice you can easily and comfortable practice in every situation. I just recommend you simplicity in every aspect of your daily life expression.

Practice

From this moment, three times a day, think about that, that there is no causation. In this moment you think like this, just stop doing things for a while, breathe slowly and feel the passion of a current moment. Now say (it is not important to express these words or not): "There is something certain in this situation. What act is here, what I want right now?"

At the end of this practice, you can do what you have to do with words: *"Here I act this situation, let's go further."* Of course, use every time your own words. The results, or fruits of this practice, will come very quickly over the next few days. You'll be amazed to see also by this practice, what you have unconsciously overlooked.

If you wish to understand unmanifested communication which is beyond causation, you have to observe actually situation and act in actually situation. Exactly, through observation and inner action, you create outer results. Everything that you are now is a result of actions already taken, so to be where you want to be, you have to know what actions you need to take. Here are some steps that you can take in this process of observing and acting.

First step is self-observation. This is why you need to continually transform old habits to consciousness. There's one rule I've noticed with my clients and other people. What you observe, does not like when it is observed. This means that if you observe something, it becomes more and more confidential for you or in other words, by observing you get answers about the nature of the observed.

Self-observation leads to the understanding of mental behavior patterns and understanding of mental behavior patterns leads to self-knowing.

Second step is certainty of expression. Certainty of expression is ruled of cause and effect. Cause and effect, as you already know, occurs only by one accepting the laws of social system. However, in order to re-enforce success in your hands, you need to understand the rules of causality. For every action, there are a specific results.

Third step is, that effects are every time greater than the cause. Many mistakenly believe that they will receive the same as they sent. Have in mind, that every cause produces awesome results. The question is, in what direction is the awesome result. How do these consequences grow? It's simple. According to the law of similarity, where similar attracts similar. This means that all kinds of similar causal situations are constantly connected and when the right circumstances have occurred, they all have been a huge and awesome consequence.

Take always only those actions which are according of this questions:

1. Is it joyful?
2. Is it helpful?
3. Is it successful?

You have to also know, that you never received the consequence without committing the cause.

Fourth step is, that there is possibility to transform already performed cause. Many trainers or coaches teach that the cause cannot be erased and changed, but I will tell you that it is possible. If that wouldn't be possible, then all the teachings about being the creators of your happiness and misfortune would be wrong and untrue.

Instead of self-blaming, self-humiliating, self-ashamed and all those negative self-feelings that cause self-destructive consequences, take that as well as it is. Just say *"This is the best way, it can be."* and *"I do everything in the best way I can."* You have to be reconciled with your relative past, so that you can create your relative future from the current moment. Closing the peace or be in harmony with your relative past is the essence of this point of teaching. If you don't do it, you will only collect all causes that must occur by the law of similarity.

Unmanifested communication is beyond time, space and causation and you've seen, how simple and easy is to understand it, without thousands of theories and speculations.
Here is one practice you can also easily and comfortable practice in every moment. You can play with it, how you like. I just recommend you be simple in every aspect of your daily life expression.

Practice
From this moment, whenever in you occur questions in sense like "how... why... what...", breathe slowly and say (it is not important to express these words or not): *"What is that what I want right now?"*
At the end of this practice, you can do what you have to do with words: *"Here I am, let's go further."* Of course, use every time your own words.

Manifested communication

"Change your word and you change the world."

Manifested communication is the place, where your successful journey already is. This is first place or the place of beginning, where "thoughts, words and acts" occurred. Yet, also here at the beginning of manifestation are all thoughts, words and acts structured inside you. At the moment of reaching a sufficient amount of information, the thoughts are appeared. At the moment of reaching a sufficient amount of thoughts, the words - internal communication - are appeared. At the moment of reaching a sufficient amount of words, the acting - internal actions - is appeared. These thoughts, words and actions are happening at once. In other words, there is no difference inside you between those three powers. Finally, at the moment of reaching a sufficient amount of thoughts, words and actions - internal creating process - , manifested communication in duality (world around you) appeared.

There are three wonderful powers behind this internal process. Without these three powers, there is no creative communication, no creative actions and no success. These three powers are *1. Affirmation* (positive system of creating success), *2. Negation* (negative system of creating success), *3. Conciliation* (neutral or harmonizing system of creating success). How can you understand it? Imagine how the two magnets are connected. For example, if you group 2 magnets with a diameter of 12mm and a thick 3mm, these magnets together will hold a magnet power of

12mm in diameter and 6mm thick. Therefore, by grouping information values (positive and negative), we achieve that thoughts, words and actions are grouped and multiplied and have power as a one larger unit – your success.

Now you have to understand the process of creating success in manifested communication. When you read this, you can have a lot of questions. But don't worry. Here is explanation how you can conquer this three powers of creating success on the field of the manifested communication.

You have to begin with the third power – *conciliation*. Conciliation is neutral or harmonizing system of creating every success. You have your own experience and your own knowledge the knowing that in order to create, you have to combine some possibilities. Only by combining has made everything that has happened to this moment.

For an even better understanding of this description, I invite you to do the following practice.

Practice

Imagine a situation where you have come to a particular solution by combining different options. This may be a job search situation where you considered all the advantages and opposites, or this may be the situation when choosing a school, or this may be the situation when choosing a partner or any other situation.

Write all the details of this combining process.

With the moment when you can receive, or better to say when you can be with everything with joy, gladfulness and gratitude, the second power or *negation* or negative system of creating success is occurred in you. That means to let everything as it is. Here are all the unpleasants from others and also from inside of yourself. Here is the loving of your "enemies", to love those who beat you, who hated you, who humiliated you, who underestimated you, who have refused you, who ignored you, who cursed you, who robbed you, who persecuted you, etc., so all the negative perceived situations.

To relieve the situation, I invite you to do the following practices.

Practice one
Imagine where you were confronted with some unpleasant situation, but which later turned out to be the best possible option.
Now imagine the positive outcome from that situation.
Write, how experience from that situation can help you to react in all other situations.

Practice two
One more time imagine the previous unpleasant situation.
Now change your reactions in that situation with using of joy, gladfulness and gratitude.
Write what feelings you have now.

With the moment of positive joying of every moment and every situation, the first power or *affirmation* or positive system of creating success occurred. Only observing of positive situations and by using positive thoughts, words and actions can make you successful.

This means that you can every time choose what you observe and what thoughts, words and actions you use. You have to love yourself as you are. I want to tell you, that you have to be willing to stop worrying about all unpleasant situations, thoughts, words and deeds. Just search positive propositions and be positive. Do not think about where the joy or success or all the money comes from, think about actual moment of joy. In first place should be every time joyfulness, that's essential to know it, because your first manifestation are your emotions. Everything else, in words of duality, comes after that. That is why it is necessary to have first sown and harvested positiveness. In this sense, you are always able to see your way of success. For this sense, I invite you to do the following practice.

Practice
Imagine one till three situations when you were absolutely positive and joyful and things was going so amazing, that the outcomes was behind your expectation.

Write, how beautiful it is to know, that you have in your hands all the possibilities to make that perfect outcomes in every moment.

This are the three wonderful powers behind this internal process of manifested communication. Yet, the previous descriptions are still not the end. About affirmations, negations and conciliations, I wrote all details later.

To conquer manifested communication, I let you know some more details about this process in which you can see also *constructive manifested communication* and *destructive manifested communication*. These two parts of communication are your standard conversational skills, so communication between two and more people in social system.

Constructive manifested communication

Constructive manifested communication is the possibility, where your successful journey strengthens and multiplies everything positively.

Constructive manifested communication have its own specific structure and use collection of special techniques that prioritize the mental and physical wellbeing of all participants. Using the correct technique of manifested communication permits you to arrive at the highest of all your possibilities. You should distinguish between a mind that is still and in peace and a mind that is stilled by uncontrolled need or violently silenced. When the mind is stilled by uncontrolled need or violently silenced, it is really not still and peaceful. Only still and peaceful mind can produce positiveness. When the thinking system remains under your control, success comes to you absolutely spontaneous. Don't forget, every moment is your possibility to achieve success! Therefore, when you have to talk with somebody, choose first following questions.

1. Are you absolutely sure about your truth?
2. Is it joyful, gladful and thankful?
3. Is it positive?
4. Is it on observed oriented?

If communication is already necessary, choose following techniques of communication.

"Only a mind that is at Silence, Peace and Harmony can solve all your requirements."

Using peace and silence
It's useful to not speak at all. Premeditated peace and silence give both observer and observed an opportunity to think and found the right solution. You should always let the other people the options to end peace and silence, but you should never brake the peace and silence before you don't have the absolute answer.

People talk and act only because they suffer. That's the fact. Just imagine a person who is absolutely joyful and happy. Such a person does not need to talk or act, he simply enjoys his joyfulness and satisfaction.

Example one: The causes of your suffering - whether mental or physical - cannot be found with our physical senses. Therefore, to experience the Truth is fundamental. Of course, the truth is impossible to experience in duality, because it is not a situation build out from never ending details. The Truth comes to us by means of comprehension of the peace and silence.

In the moment of conversation, you have to conquer following steps:

1. Harmonious presence
2. Harmonious gratitude
3. Harmonious attention
4. Harmonious intention
5. Harmonious effort
6. Harmonious offering
7. Harmonious posture, facial expression and gesture

Example two: I would like to tell you a story from my practice as a coach of professional athletes.

One standard training day, I was watching a practice session in the gym. I realized that the dynamic presence of the other athletes was interfering one athlete so strongly, that he couldn't do the technique in the right way. I step to him and asked: "What's the problem?" He answers: "I don't know, I cannot repeat it." I followed this conversation: "You must first understand the harmony inside you." I got an idea. From the windows of my gym you can see beautiful mountains, so I invited him to come with me to one of the windows. I have said to him: "Look at the river on the mountains, there are some rocks in its way. Is the river in some way limited by their presence? No. It simply flows over and around them and simple moves on! Let the river be your example how to be in harmony. If something disturbs you, leave it where it is, but outside of you. Concentrate only on your movements, because your technique is unique and unrepeatable. You do not worry about you, you are the expression of uniqueness. You are not all that worry around you, you are the expression of uniqueness." After three months, this athlete won his first international grappling title.

Using whole potential of relativity
Use only words that are not ruled with time, space and causation. There is one rule here how to correctly communicate. The presentation of positive information must be presented in the present time and the presentation of negative information in the past time.

Therefore, choosing words not ruled with time, space and causation is giving you direct access to the perfect solution. Communication in this sense is enormous enrichment for both observer and observed.

Example one: To conquer "whole potential of relativity", you have to first answer on following questions. Try to answer as quickly as possible, wrote it and in one year look at it one more time. You will be impressed what outcome it was for you. Of course, it is possible that you can ask someone to read these questions for you.

1. Who I am?
2. Where I am?
3. What is this situation?
4. What is this desire?
5. What is it that wants all the success, money, attention, comfort, satisfaction and acceptance?
6. Where is it that wants all the success, money, attention, comfort, satisfaction and acceptance?
7. What is the meaning of good?
8. Where is the place of good?
9. What is the meaning of bad?
10. Where is the place of bad?
11. Is this moment real?
12. How to handle?

Example two: Instead of saying, *"I am not doing well"* say *"I was not doing well"*, or instead *"He think I cannot do it"* say *"He thought about me that I could not do it"*, or *"I cannot do it"* say *"I could not do it"* and so far.

What you say to yourself or to others influences how you feel about what goes on in you and around you. Your feelings depend of course on whether you adopt a positive or negative interpretation of the situation. Therefore, your feeling and reaction should be in present time positive.

Using of focusing

Being attentive to what the others are saying, you distribute peaceful atmosphere and allow nice relaxing and contemplational conversation. The others straight see how important they are to you.

With focusing you are centered on the current detail, so your focus should be sharper than the sharpest tip, because you already change all the possible following situations in the current moment. Through this kind of concentration is your potential refined. Right now, you are challenged with your concentration. The ability to concentrate is developed according to how you use attention during your activities. There are many techniques how to train concentration, but I recommend you to make it easy. Just make it with your willpower. Concentration shouldn't be never static and tense. Just be relaxed and attentive, nothing less and nothing more.

Focusing is very effective and important at business meetings as a manipulation strategy to obtaining the necessary information.

Example: The right way to be focused contains the liberation from old habits. Here are some important old habits which should be transformed.

1. Ignorance (lack of knowing)
2. Pride, hostility and selfishness
3. Prejudices (towards yourself and others)
4. Value system and conviction
5. Distrust

Using "observe and talk" technique

Self-observation at the first place means an internal process to achieve a transformation. In this interpersonal process, you learn how to observe everything outside. True self-observation is an active process of focused attention, without the influence of your thoughts, words and actions. "Observe and talk" by constructive manifested communication means to use the right tool, at the right moment, at the right place and to the right person.

By observing you can make also short compliment in the context of the theme. Sometime is it necessary to make short and eloquent compliment. It can lead to a better atmosphere and more open conversation.

Example: To be able correct use "observe and talk", you should follow this strategy steps.

1. Say *"Thank you!"* – If someone makes you a compliment or otherwise appreciates you, every time say *"Thank you!"*. If you are not thankful, what is acknowledgment and acceptance of the appreciation, you robbed yourself at both mental and physical level.

2. Acknowledge others – If other people contributed to your achievement, then give them a positive and thankful feedback. For example *"I am grateful to my parents and friends who have been very helpful in achieving this success."*

3. Be specific – Instead *"Great work today!"*, feel following sentence *"Today, you have done a really great job with the necessary information values."*
4. Be focused – Instead *"You look good"*, feel following sentence *"You look really good today, what is the secret behind it?"*.
5. Smile – Smile is the simplest thing you can give. If you try to smile every hour for some seconds, you will see big change in your life immediately.

Using empathy

Your ability to understand another person's situation and feelings, bring you on higher level of competency. Empathy includes the ability to listen. Empathic listening is not about agreeing, it is about seeing yourself, other persons or things as they are. Listening is for others an indication that we understand them, that we do care about them and that we have understanding for them from what they are saying.

Example: For better empathy, I recommend you following steps.

1. Put aside your point of view and see the person or current situation as it is.
2. Pay attention physically and mentally, to what's happening.
3. Be instinctive and flexible.
4. Validate the other person's perspective and ask what the other person would do.

Using hope

Hope is something as enormous as the being itself. Encouragement must be perfect timed and must be every time in positive sense. In this days is encouragement maybe the biggest tool to safe someone life and bring him on the path, where he want to be.

Example one: At first, answer on following questions.

1. What's the most emotive you've ever lost, what did you really care about?
2. How did you feel?
3. How did you deal with this loss?

Example two: Now you have to choose. "TRY" or "DO"? I encourage you, every time to "DO". Never "try" something, because if you go to "try", you are satisfied with failure.

Instead to say *"I will try to exercise for better health"* say *"I do exercise for health"*, or instead to say *"I will try to give up smoking"* say *"I do better things than smoking"*, or instead to say *"I will try some business"* say *"I do business in my own way and that's great"* and so on.

Example three: Now you have to choose second time. "MUST" or "CAN"? Never say "I must", because as by "try", you are also satisfied with failure.

Instead to say *"I must try to exercise for better health"* say *"I can exercise for health"*, or instead to say *"I must to give up smoking"* say *"I can give up smoking"*, or instead to say *"I must try to do some business"* say *"I can do business in my own way and that's great"* and so on.

If I use the word "must" or other command words in this book, I only use them to emphasize the significance of the theme. Every time have in your mind the one and only powerful statement "I CAN" instead I MUST", because you really CAN DO whatever you want and you must do nothing.

Using of humor

Humor presented at the right time, in the right place and to the right person, activates the body's special natural adaptation mechanisms.

Humor must be perfectly timed because it is a two-dimensional option. As he can help, he can also destroy everything.

Example one: In the sense of a better understanding of humor, answer the following questions.

1. What joke do you want to hear three minutes before you die?
2. What speech would you put on your own funeral?
3. What joke do you want to hear about yourself, three years after your death?

Example two: Let´s talk about structure of a humor.

1. Set-up of humor – beginning of humor according to the current mental and physical status of the situation;

2. Anchor on the situation – determine how the audience should feel;
3. Moment of magnificence – the very manifestation of humor and a decent abandon of humor

Using analogies and metaphors

With using of analogies and metaphors you're no longer bound by the boundaries of the duality. Instead of it, you work on solving the current situation by act with the analogies and metaphors in imagination.

This effective method of creating encourage you and others to think outside the duality.

Example one: Here is a structure for correct using of analogies and metaphors.

1. Initiation – you have to know, what an information values you would like to give observers;
2. Induct emotional states of interest – you should attract the attention of observers;
3. The very theme – the theme must be eloquent and result oriented;
4. Outcome – t he outcome must be always refreshing and nourishing;

Example two: The following structure is geared to concrete speeches of analogies and metaphors.

1. Thank the observers;
2. Start and be positive;
3. Refer to current situation;

4. Give hope;
5. Make a strong statement;
6. Be patient;
7. Use peaceful gestures;
8. Let the observers talk each other;

Using alternate perspective

At any moment, you have lots of possibilities. You have only to choose the right tool for them. Alternative perspective is one of such possibilities to make, for example, from one business many more business in one line.

In the process of forming communication, clarifying values and taking an strategic position, the observers considers different ways of looking at situations and reaching possible solutions. Well and in such situations, this alternate perspective is a valuable tool.

Example: Alternate perspective use following steps to reach the right solution.

1. Introduce observers the multiple sides of situations.
2. Invite observers to gather, access and compare information values.
3. Invite observers to take an action.
4. Include frequent opportunities for reflection.
5. After consideration of alternate perspectives, require observers to clarify their own current positions.
6. Support them with their new position.

Using importance

When you faced an unpleasant situation it was easy to become overwhelmed with all the details. You should not want an immediate result just by snap your finger. You are in process. That's like if you wanted to stop a car with a power of will. For this moment, let the details be as they are and relax. Let the situation flow. The solution of these situation is coming in the moment of focusing for the importance of relaxing.

You know, with big problems come big solutions. But the big solutions occur only in relaxing body and mind.

Example: In the moment of current situation (pleasant or unpleasant), take these questions:

1. Here is something important right now.
2. What did I think about at this moment?
3. What did I talking about at this moment?
4. What I get at this moment?
5. Let's get further.

Using of providing the necessary information

Always provide only the necessary information, but formulate it as something extra. Your listener must have the impression that you are giving him something more as standard. This is how also modern marketing work.

Sometimes you don't need to change concept of your presentation, just try in another way to formulate the name of presentation.

Example: Following changing business information strategy can help you change your past to become successful with an already exist projects.

   1. Create a requirement in the world – The most important part of selling is understanding the needs of your customers. The most important thing everyone needs is valuable information. Valuable information must include:
- Introduction of information
- Specification
- Timing
- Speed, Repeating and Multiplying
- There is no end, only flowing beginnings of never ending possibilities
   2. Know the borderless of information – The information must be borderless, so the customer should see his unlimited possibilities. How to refer one´s full potential include following steps:
- Setting one´s potential as a success
- Set inspiration
- Set "as if" effect
- Set intuition effect
- Set "moving on, moving forward" effect
   3. Address the "human side" systematically – Systematic influence of the emotional component of the mind of the consumers is an option that gives you the opportunity to be extraordinary. In this

sense, it is necessary to control many communication techniques. The Law of manipulative communication include combinations (which must be constantly changed) from following three steps:

- Good or pleasant communication
- Bad or unpleasant communication
- Neutral or observed communication

4. Create ownership – Ownership is the expression of yourself. It is such a powerful expression that can never be confused with any other expression. Look at the biggest companies or religions of this planet. If you hear their slogans, you can never confuse them with any other company or religion.

5. Create multicultural message – The multicultural message must be unambiguous. The multicultural language is, for example, health, money or education.

6. Prepare others for unexpected – In order to prepare someone for something unexpected, you should include some precise direction in your campaign.
   Take following steps in your strategy:

- Show faith
- Show another perspective
- Use the multiplicity of meanings
- Use your own words

7. Speak to the individual – With "speak to the individual" you have the keys from the houses of your

customer. How is it possible? Simple. The interest itself is confirmation of entry.

Using of clarification

Clarification is a way to further clarify what you have already said. It is important in many situations, especially when what is being communicated is difficult to understand in some way. This is an important way to show your competence. It looks like banality, but in the hands of an experienced speaker, it is a powerful tool to transform a good situation into a perfect one.

Example: Clarification have its own structure.

1. Reinterpretation with a new aspect
2. Speed
3. Give example
4. Be specific
5. Raise the theme to a higher level

Using the correct questions

I always say *"Where there are no questions, there are no answers."* You have to use the correct questions and to ask correct questions is in one hand with correct answers the highest communication tool. Everyone who have answers is a ruler of current situation and ruler of the whole success.

Example: Using the correct questions and answers have its own structure:

1. In the right time

2. On the right place
3. To the right person

Using "it is as it is" attitude

By taking your own attitude "It is as it is", you express absolute satisfaction at every moment. "It is as it is" can bring you out from any unpleasant situation. This is not only a big statement, this is the way of life.

Example: Try to feel this statement: *"All I have to do should be just letting all that frustration, anger and fight outside me and just letting it as it is. Let's go further."*

Using self-offering

Many situations seemed very stressful. You could feel in them lonely, sad, angry and hopeless. That's how also others could feel in their situations. It's not a good and positive experience. But you can change it right now.

Using self-offering doesn't mean, that you should offer your body or spirit in some ritual. Self-offering means, that you should see the positive outcome of any situation, which made you uncomfortable.

Example: Instead of regretting someone else, imagine him instantly as a joyful, satisfied and happy person. That's the best and highest gift you can offer to someone. No material thank offering is equal to this wonderful internal act.

Using "open the door" technique

Constructive manifested communication is often most effective when others can lead the flow of communication and decide what to talk about.

The "open the door" technique lets you stay in the role of an observer while allowing others to show their inner attitudes.

Example: The doorway to knowledge is what we all seek. To knock on that doorway, you have to know where it is. The doorway is within yourself. If you ignore yourself with all the negative thinking, or if you are ignoring what is happening in your mind, you are closing the door.

Therefore I often say *"It is necessary to know and not only to believe."* So how you can use the "open the door" technique? With your presence, with your presentation skills, with your whole personality. You are the "opened door itself."

Using "place a new element" technique

"Placing a new element" is a technique that is timeless. When you place a new element in communication, you are opened something that is bigger than you and whole communication, in which you had the element placed. It can help get a clearer sense of the whole theme or situation, but it can lead to absolutely another theme or situation. Using "placing a new element" technique requires a real knowledge of the current theme or situation.

Example: The new element you can place with help of following structure.

1. New idea
2. Encoding of idea
3. New value of idea

Using of winning confrontation

Sometimes confrontation is inevitable. For this reason, it is necessary to be a winner before each situation. You are constantly the winner and you also have to act from this point of view. Just establish trust. Well-timed confrontation (at the right time, at the right place and the right person) can help break destructive habits or understand the state of the situation.

To use winning confrontation is a big strategy tool, which can make you very successful person.

Example: Every time you have someone in front of you, you must see how to positively influence them. That's the essence. Make them a little more smile and immediately you made a positive influence. You have to change everything into creating the best possible results.

Using of feedback

Mastering of a feedback should be your big secret weapon. Feedback is not just a coaching tool, it is the art of showing your absolute competence. With this powerful tool, you get instant confidence from observers and become a "mentor-father/mother".

Example: To mastering feedback, you need perfect structure of it and this is one of my favorite structures I use.

1. Take the best strategic position of your body in the space – choose the best place to react.
2. Be focused and patient – use the perfect timing.
3. Transform / Manipulate space (changing body language) – with perfect timing use the possibility to change your position in space. The listener should to see your movement.
4. Before you start with your feedback, create safety atmosphere – first you should thank the listener for the possibility to give him a feedback. This should not be too emotional and you should use a moderate voice.
5. Before you start with your feedback, establish the purpose of the following conversation – put yourself in the position of a helper, not a "striker". Feedback should be opened to all sides.
6. Start – start calmly, but purposefully, with a constant focus on the listener.
7. Describe first the positive behavior and explain the importance or impact of this behavior – a positive start will ease the situation and prepare you for the most important aspects of feedback.
8. Focus on improvement instead of criticism – an offer to improve is to open the door to further communications and provide the listener with a new insight into the situation.

9. Formulate your observation as a message – put the listener in the position that he is already on the way of the desired situation. Feel this statement *"Make a small change of your expressive abilities and you can go easily on the stage as a speaker."* After using this sentence, my listener decided to go on stage (after two weeks) and became a successful speaker.
10. Be specific and immediate – quick reactions in the feedback boost the desired feedback effect.
11. Use pauses – using pause allows you to refresh your communication and to involve the listener in the process.
12. Use PCM technique – PCM (power of constructive manipulation) is a technique that I have developed to make the listener go constantly beyond his imaginative boundaries. PCM is very useful technique, which award the listener for the current moment.
13. Give smile and big THANK YOU! – This is a very powerful confirmation of everything you said and at the same time triggering a better perspective for the listener. It has to be very emotional statement with big gestures and with an increasing tone of voice, which ends with your focused direct look into the eyes of the listener.

Using tone of voice

Each moment has its own frequency and only an experienced strategist can feel it and use this frequencies in its own benefit.

Your voice change the "reality", so you are able to change every communication how you like. You can influence others to tune them to your frequency. Once you've tuned someone to your frequency, you begin to create all potential future situations.

You have to be very careful, what tone of voice do you choose and at what occasion. To know is the difference between success and failure.

Example: Try modifying your tonality by controlling its elements.

1. Voice Tone (high, low or other)
2. Tempo (slow, fast or other)
3. Timbre (clear, raspy or other)
4. Volume (loud, soft or other)

Using of postures and gestures

The most underestimated and misunderstood component of communication are postures and gesticulations. If you look around, you will see the madness of posturing and gesticulating. It is incredible how many unnecessary movements the persons around you are constantly doing.

You must use peaceful and harmony postures and gestures that are always in the context of how you communicate.

You have to also know, that the postures and gesticulation are a tool how to turn all situation to your advantage. Well-timed posture and gesticulation (in the right time, at the right place and to the right person) can help to break potential failure and lead to your victory.

Example: Correct way of postures and gestures have following steps.

Postures
1. Open
2. Straight
3. Relaxed
4. Harmonious with concept of speech, space and current situation

Gestures
1. Open
2. Relaxed
3. Harmonious with concept of speech, space and current situation

Using of summarizing

Summarization is a tool that gives all participants a chance to have a sense in understanding. It is a short recapitulation and recapitulation is also a retrospection in which it is possible to modify all relative past situations. With this tool you can see all the communication or work already done.

Example: When you finish the retrospection, you have already recognized a series of events that happened to you during concrete process and which are related to different mental situations. These include, for example, fear, anger, ambition, inattention, pride, snappishness, etc. This is why the retrospection is the first step you should do when you want to go from place you are to the place where you want to be.

Use of confidentiality
This is the most significant and essential aspect of constructive manifested communication. Confidentiality is something so extremely intimate, that it cannot be overtaken by even the communication itself. Confidentiality cannot be learned. Either it is in you or not.

To conquer the constructive manifested communication you must to adhere to the rules of intimacy and that's the confidentiality.

Example: Look around you a say "There is nothing I cannot keep confidential." You can use the following steps to improve this intimate ability.

1. As the highest priority you should set your self-awareness, self-knowledge and self-realization.
2. Be quiet and peaceful.
3. Do not share your daily life with others and use the possibility „*Where there are no questions, there are no answers."*
4. Be intuitive and conscious.
5. Use discretion when discussing confidential information.

6. Protect intellectual property of others and inform your clients how their information are used.
7. Use different kinds of strategies to make the privacy information safe.

As you can see, constructive manifested communication is not just a simple communication skill, about this kind of communication you have to take care of. Caring the essence of relationship in the constructive manifested communication, must be forefront in determining of all kind of communication.

Destructive manifested communication
Destructive manifested communication is the possibility, where your successful journey weakens and multiplies everything negatively. Here are all your communications habits that hold you back and outside of success.
Destructive manifested communication haw no structure. Destructive communication is all that communication, which is not under control.
Once you ware active in this present world, other people has thrown all kinds of possibilities at you. What the others throws at you is determined by your conviction of accepting and what you made out of it is still up to you.
But how to deal with destruction and negative forces? Make a distinction between the nature of "who you are" and the nature of "who are the others". This distinction you can make only by following the truth. When I talk

about truth, I don't talk about your convictions, I talk about the "seeing everything as it is". If you really want be there where you want to be, you must do what works and you must give this knowing further, because everyone wants to be happy.

There are a lot of possibilities to invest in, but you should never invest in other's problems, never ever. That's the rule No1 before all rules in success strategy. If you can change your mindsets, if you make a fundamental change in the way you perceive, understand and experience daily life, whole population will change. Yes, you can do it! Be courageous and just change your mindset.

Every time you meet someone, you have to see him as he is and how to positively influence him. The least you can do, is to give him a little smile. With smile you influence him on mental and neuronal level and the effect of this gesture will stay in him lifelong.

Destructive manifested communication was around you in every day activities. If you are active in the social system, with this type of communication you will continue to meet. It's just so. But, if you can be with situations without being affected by them, you become a creator of your own daily life situations. You have to know, that the outer situations don't decide who you naturally are but you decide how the situations were, are and will be. You can call it as a freedom, joyfulness, happiness, lucky, pleasure, knowing, success, or as you wish.

Chapter two

"Going beyond resolutions is a state of creating."

WILLPOWER AND DESIRE FOR SUCCESS
"Your willpower and desire are bigger than the mind itself"

In the beginning of this chapter, I give you one question:

"If you believe in achieving your goal, if you can imagine your goal, if you can feel your goal, do you need constantly ask for it?"

You know the questions like "When will I finally be successful?" or "How do I achieve my dream success?" You also know the answers like "Don´t worry, be happy." or "Don´t worry, everything is fine." or "Think positive." or "Live here and now in the present moment."
The reason these people have lost line to their life success is that they focused only on what is good or positive for them. They want everything right here and right now, regardless of the circumstances. They want it only with the positive thinking. Such a way of thinking has caused many individuals and families great existential problems. Where is the problem of such of thinking? The greatest problem of all goodness or positivity is its relativity. To be positive, one should know its concept and this concept is described in the reality of willpower and desire – the positive and the negative aspect of creating.

Before I introduce you one structure that can help you to use the positively thinking correctly, let us talk about value of unpleasant situations. The value of the unpleasant situation is as high as you allow it to be. If you're dealing with the unpleasant situations with most of your daily attention, you're automatically giving it priority – high value. The priority of all situations is multiplied by the daily attention you pay for it. That's the rule, that's the law, that's how its work. What you can do is to let the unpleasant situation grow into its absolute size, because as you already know, big problems bring great answers. Let it grow and go relax how you like. You can relax while sleeping, eating, reading, walking, or other situation in which you can be in the state of "no-thinking". Just relax and let everything else be as it is. After your relaxing situation, the answer with solution can occur and you will know when, where and how. But do not be hasty to think about the unpleasant situation, because the backward problem oriented hastiness is a support of the current and following unpleasant situations. Have it in your mind, because a lot of people stay in the unpleasant situations many days, years or whole lifetime. Now you are ready to take and use the following structure, which can help you to use the positive thinking correctly.

1. Get relief from the current situation
2. Accept the situation as it is
3. Relax
4. Take action to go further

As support to everything written, there is one big possibility – affirmations. Affirmations are wonderful and powerful support to prepare you for wanted and desired success. Using of affirmations in the right or correct way have also its own structure, as everything in the process of becoming joyful and successful person.

There are three wonderful powers, as you already know, behind internal process of creating. Without these three powers, there is no creative communication, no creative actions and no success. This wonderful powers are the affirmation, the negation and the conciliation. To make these three great powers point to what you really want, there are another two powers that you need to know and use firstly. Those powers are willpower and desire. About desire I written something small, but here I going to explain it more detailed.

Willpower and desire are two powers of one and only concept. Willpower we can analogically describe as a positive power and desire as a negative. From this start line you have to know, that the willpower is not a desire and the desire is not a willpower. They work together, but you can work with them also separately. If you worked with them separately, of course you got an unpleasant situations as a result. This goes especially for the one-way use of desire – the negative one, the unconscious use of positiveness in inappropriate manner, at the wrong time, on the wrong place, in the wrong situation and to the wrong person. The desire expressed in the position of lack, sadness, anger and frustration is the multiplier of the current flourishing situation.

Willpower is that power that you have to improve in order to achieve your success. This is very important to understand, because all success relies on willpower. This is the only work, you have to do. Improve willpower skills. To improve the willpower is necessary to learn how. The whole concept of willpower is the taking of responsibility for your life. You can use following formulation: *"I took responsibility for my life."* It is such a huge and powerful statement that its reach cannot be sufficiently described. With this statement you take under your control the responsibility for your thoughts, words, feelings and actions. You take under your control the whole nature. With this statement you should be free from collective beliefs. You alone is enough for your success. You don't need to take the opinions of others. Their minds are related with the social and many others laws. You are exceptional individual, so do not bring into your home unnecessary conviction of others. That's you biggest possibility you have. If you can keep this huge and powerful statement daily on your mind, your life will change rapidly.

After you took responsibility for your life, you have to practice patience. Patience is not something that you can learn quickly. The ability to be patient is something that has nothing to do with the time assumption. It has nothing to do with a standard social instinct. To be patient is to know that all people and all situations are so as they are.

In one hand with the patience, you must to transform your social instincts, your whole belief system into intuition. This transformation you can call also as a switch, because in the true sense it is only something like imaginary bridge between two systems – belief system and intuition. This switch or imaginary bridge is your observation. Well that's exactly the way you improve or also train your willpower. Willpower is you real consciousness, your individuality. The willpower or your consciousness or your individuality, is still tested and that's good. That's the straight way you can see your transformation or progress to your success. If you act with your willpower in the relative wrong way, with desire, is because you was identified with another belief system.

In addition to understanding and practicing the above mentioned processes, the following system can help you increase your willpower and desire in the right and natural way.

1. Encourage yourself to take an action – Trust in your abilities and act as soon as you have an impulse. By taking the action, you have taken all the following situations into your own hands. Even by reading this book, you have created an action that results in your satisfaction and success.
2. Use stretching and meditation every day – These two methods are enriching each other and therefore their regular practice gives you immediate results.

3. Eat the right way – for example, by finding out (natural observing of yourself) what makes for you healthy and satisfied benefit and what don't.
4. Change your comfort habits – for example, use every day also your opposite hand, or wake up one minute earlier, or drink one coffee less than normal and so on. This creates a discomfort for the learned and subconsciously adopted habits, which automatically leads to your personal development.
5. Manage your speech – for example, use more positive and empathy words (amazing, understanding, joyful, helpful, great, confident, impressive, splendid, etc.) and stop to use insignificant words (oe, hmm, oi, hey, etc.), or stop to use derogative and swear words, or stop to use negations ("I cannot", "It´s impossible", "I have no chance", etc.).
6. Act simple – for example, identify something easy and small every day and do it in easiest way as you can. Don't think about details, just do it in easiest way.
7. Use "There are only possibilities" strategy – do not have time to deal with problems, focus on what makes you happy and that there are never ending possibilities in every situation.

Now you know, why it is so important to take responsibility for your life and you know how to handle it.

Happily and with pleasure we get to the actual process of the three wonderful powers and how to use them for your success.

Willpower and desire, which are behind these powers, we can describe as an intention. Intention, by this meaning, is indescribable, because each from us have its own intentions for billions of situations in every second. That's the fact. The form that is given to that power depends on the direction given to it by the one making the intention. It is not just a simple idea that "I'd like achieve something" and if I do a little prayer practice it will come for alone only so. This is real science, not a street joke. This is so mighty and beautiful concept of creating, that all other tools seem before him like a children. This concept is stronger than matter and with correct using you can achieve with it something that seems impossible to attain.

Allow yourself to become the inspiration of your quest for upliftment of daily life routine. Do not waste the power of intention (willpower and desire) to get rid yourself of trifling habits or egoistical passions, because those smallnesses will naturally fall away as your intention becomes a daily reality in your life.

In order not to be too mysterious here, I will introduce you more concrete steps to get from the point where you are, to the point where you want to.

You should firstly find your personal intention. Intention is not oriented toward a relative future outcome. Instead, it is a knowing that is focused on how you are manifested in the present moment. You should follow the following structure so that you do not get into mistake or information confusion.

1. Choosing of intention
2. Repeating of intention
3. Let the intention flow in its natural way

Give yourself so much time as you need to decide upon your intention, because once you have done that process, it should not be changed until it becomes a reality in your life.

When looking for an intention, you must be brief, concise, amazed and joyous of that situation. Have in the mind also, you should not deal it to anyone. It's your intimacy.

To be sure with your selection and to become the best possible answer, you can use the following inner remembering technique.

"I know that I am part of the one and only source. I know I'm unique. I know, this is my amazing body. With pleasure I receive a clear conversation about my intention. I love and follow this conversation."

With these statement you choose your intention. Now pay attention, because there must be only one intention at any one time! That´s why you have to really carefully decide, whether it is to be a short-term or a long-term intention.

Go beyond your intellect, because this practice have nothing to do with your intellect. In this practice is your intellect undesirable and can have unwanted or destructive effect. Also, intention can no one choose for you. It is your personal possibility.

You should know that the answer can be anything. Just let the answer come. This type of answer can help you in all life situations and when I say in all, I mean in all. With it you can achieve the impossible things.

At the moment of receiving the intention after practice the above-mentioned technique, it is necessary to make a conscious act of gratitude.

"I am fully aware of this wonderful conversation, for which I am grateful that it happened."

After these necessary and important acceptance gratitude, your first statement on very beginning, your first intention in the process of becoming successful, should be:

"I found my Intention."

When you are satisfied with your intention, it is ready to be utilized as a construct or a goal, to give you a positive direction to your success.

During the recitation of the completed intention (construct), you should be in peace and harmony, but filled with joy, satisfaction, amazement, that is, be simply in harmony with your whole sincere energy. Such a powerfully created intention transform whole life experience, which is often called as a destiny.

To strengthen the intention, it can be repeated, in accordance with the rule of a correct time, place and situation. Repeating the intention should always be in harmony with your whole sincere energy, as I wrote. You can repeat it at the beginning and at the end of your daily routine. For example, you can repeat it before you go to sleep and then one more time repeat it, when you wake up, or you can repeat it before you go to meditate and then one more time after the meditation techniques and so on.

Once you have decided for your concrete intention, never have any doubts about it. Always be positive and trustful towards your intention. This leads to the harmonious flow in its natural way.

What can help you in your daily practice, is the following inner remembering technique.

"I am a valuable and unique being. I am a clear beneficiary of well-being. All satisfaction and joyfulness are always on my way. Everything that I do is changing to my abundance and success. Glory and eternal joyfulness are my nature. I love to be who I am, I love to be where I am. I am who I am, thus I enable all to be who they are. I am the source of everything.
Hallelujah, Hallelujah, Hallelujah."

As I wrote, the support to everything written, there is one big possibility – affirmations. Affirmations, with negations and conciliations are a unity process. Therefore, all your affirmations must be in harmony with the components of negation and conciliation.

Once you have created your intention, you can prepare yourself to start with the affirmations. As preparation to start with the affirmations serves the following rule. You must acquire this rule and not neglect it in any way. This rule is an imaginary bridge between successful and unsuccessful use of the affirmation process. In the great pleasure I introduce you now the important and essential steps to succeeding through affirmations.

"Before you begin to affirm, enjoy the current moment by loving everything. Let everything be as it is. Just be in peace, silence and harmony. Thus you are instantly tuned with the principle of creation."

Enjoying the current moment by loving everything is an energetic fuel in whole creating process. This energetic fuel helps you seeing everything as it is and to be in peace, silence and harmony.

As we walk on the path towards fulfill of success, we find that we must make many changes in our daily lives. Some are very subtle while others are extremely radical. One of the possibilities to make any change in your daily life, is the proper nourishment of your mental health. This nourishment is the enjoying of the current moment by loving everything.

Here are three steps to develop the described nourishment:

1. recognize that energy;
2. direct the energy by the willpower;
3. use the energy for others too;

"I recognized this energy, which is behind the enjoying of the current moment by loving everything. With my willpower I use this energy for my success and in this way I am able to make successful any other people."

Can you see it? Can you comprehend it? These aspects or steps are not separate. They work in every moment as one. This is no more just a physical concept or some kind of belief. This is how the energies work in you. If you are conscious of these facts, you are become an absolutely different person. This is because you have begun to become very serious in your daily life living. You become an observer, how you still act with yourself or with other people, how you use your speech and whole communication, how you use your mind and so on. In doing so, you are radiate another kind of life forces and the others must ask "What is it, that you do and I do not?" But, this is not simply kind of some social empathy or love. If you comprehend it, you know it and if you know it, you are acting with conscious love or with the love of wisdom. Love of wisdom is a change of your mind at all its levels. Therefore again, you have to know and not just think that you know.

Now that you already know, there is another imaginary step in the imaginative sequence of creating what you really want.

"Ask and act with the expectation of consent."

Since affirmations, negations and conciliations work as one, it is necessary to use all your formulations simple as possible and with containing these three forces at once. There is one rule about it:

"If you think about the future, it will stay as a future. If you think about past, it will stay as a past, but with possibility to change it. If you thing in present time, it is already your present time and what's more, it will be your relative future."

To make these sentences simpler and practically enforceable, here's an example.

"Once you know, you feel and you see that the willing and desired situation you have been asking for is going to be your reality, confirm it with a sentence:

That's what I want right now."

All the thoughts, words and actions that you have been heading to this moment, which is your relative future, have joined together and brought exactly what you want.

The same goes also when you face an unpleasant situation. Here is an example.

"If you face a situation or a person you do not feel well with, praise yourself for having noticed it and say to yourself:

There's something very important out here, what is it exactly, what I want right now?"

In this way, you can act in any perceived unpleasant situations and your life will change quickly.

You see, everything you need for your succeeding in you daily life, is your body. You've already read so much articles, you've been on so many seminars and trainings, you've already practiced so much, you've fallen in love so many times, you've asked so many times for what belongs to you. For what was it good if you must still searching for answers outside yourself?

When you ask and act with the expectation of consent in correct way, you can have anything you want and you can be anything you want to be. There are no limits of receiving and giving. It is an incredible statement, but it is also truthful statement. In your body you have everything you need. Take care of it and stop destroying it with social limiting beliefs. Don't put mess into it.

Be in silence and peace and just relax, because tension can destroy your body. There are another three rules, how your life with help of your body works.

1. To achieve everything you want, your body and mind must cooperate. They must be in harmony. In other words, your body and mind must be strong.
2. If your body is stronger than your mind, you will not succeed.
3. If your mind is stronger than your body, you will not succeed.

For a better understanding of these three rules, I will give you an example. There are many people who have some physical disability and yet are successful. How is it possible? Does not that mean, that they have a weak body and strong mind? For sure not. What happens in such case, is that they have the ability to be in the right time, at the right place and with the right situation in perfect harmony. They are in the necessary harmony. They knowingly or unknowingly work on radical change of their attitude. Yes and that's the most radical life change you need to make – to change your attitude. Change how you handle with external situations and that change begins inside you.
You must to see this world from another perspective. Not from sick or disabled perspective, but as an activated space that is ready to be transformed.

Be still in another perspective. Be in your perspective, because no one else can see, what you can see. All of you can sense and be aware of a thought, so why don't use it in its natural way? Just help your body to work as natural as possible.

You can help your body, for example, with a good start of your day with following predestination sentence, which is very popular among my clients and friends:

"Let this day be a happy and joyfully day of the birth of my abundance, which builds freedom, joy, wisdom, unity, health and satisfaction to me and to all beings."

Here we get to the point when affirmations (A), negations (N) and conciliations (C) work as one. To set a perfect ANC statement, you should sensitively consider your words with thinking on its *form*, *content* and *use*. These three beautiful ANC powers create anew. But if you do not direct them to exactly one particular point, the result is not what you expected. Therefore you have to use all your potential to direct them to exactly one particular point. That's the only way they can create immediately. One of such powerful ANC statement is:

"We are everlasting and I am confirmation of that."

Why is these statement so powerful? The reason why that statement is so powerful, is as follow:

- *We are everlasting* = because we do not exist for ourselves;
- *I am confirmation of that* = because I acknowledge that I am part of eternity (as an everlasting process) and I acknowledge that I am unique and unrepeatable;

Following scheme show you, where to find the three beautiful powers in these statement:

- *We are everlasting* = positive power (affirmation);
- *and* = neutral power (conciliation);
- *I am its confirmation* = negative power (negation);

You can also go to a greater philosophical depth in these statement as follow:

*"**We are** (positive power or affirmation) **is connected** with **I am** (negative power or negation) in order **to create** (neutral power or conciliation) everything I want."*

Another powerful ANC statement, towards to the point of strengthening "I am" affirmation, can be:

"I am successful and abundance is my nature."

*"**I am** (positive power or affirmation) **is connected** with **my nature** (negative power or negation) in order **to create abundance** (neutral power or conciliation)."*

As you already know, to set a perfect ANC statement, you should sensitively consider your words with thinking on its *form*, *content* and *use*. Each statement contains them based on your deepest feelings, which are indescribable.

In the deepest philosophical assumption of this concept of creation, it is necessary to realize that each of the three powers of creation contains all next powers at once.

- Affirmation contains negation and conciliation;
- Negation contains affirmation and conciliation;
- Conciliation contains affirmation and negation;

For this reason, you need to know what you are asking for and why. Of course you do not need to ask yourself questions such as "am I doing it right?" or "what if I don't do it in the right way?" In such a way you would only support the exact opposite of what you want to achieve. Everything you do, you do it in the best way you know. And that's the truth in current time and space.

Once you have made a powerful statement, you have to use next three powers, which are *1. Imagination* (receiving the information value from the inside), *2. Inspiration* (handling the information value received from inside) and *3. Intuition* (handling with knowing without any need for reasoning – absolute trust to yourself). These three powers or forces are a necessity in the process of creation. All your powers or forces you have within are the way to encourage you to arrive at your own understanding.

Let's take a look at these three next powers in more detail so that you can handle them correctly. You already know that the so called "correct handling" goes hand in hand with your current knowledge. Knowledge itself is already the action.

You have the tool that you need to unlock the doors of your suffering. In fact, you alone are the one who crafted your suffering doors. Once you know it and once you have made your personal and powerful statement, you have to use at first the power of Imagination.

Imagination is to receive an information value from the inside.

Example: Before you came up with an idea, there was an irresistible and indescribable feeling. At this point you got an idea or conception. This means, that before appearing of their concretion in your physical reality, any idea or concept already exists in the internal reality. Everything that has not been manifested yet exists in your inner reality. At that point when you got an idea or conception, you start to imagine them. With this imagination you make them concrete in your physical reality.

In this way, it is very easy to explain also the whole concept of relativity. Power of imagination is beyond memory and therefore is it not a fictive or fantasy mystification. Imagination is not a transformation of memory for something specific. What you have in your memory belongs only to your memory. Imagination is beyond fantasy.

Once you know it and once you have made your personal experience with the imagination, you are going to use the power of inspiration.

Inspiration is the ability to recognize information values or inner messages from your imagination.

Example: If you can interpret the symbolic images of the internal reality, you are able to receive and seeing the endless possibilities. These endless possibilities give you the opportunity to change your current reality, to the reality, where you want to be!

Interpretations of information values from inner inspiration work on the basis of identity and analogy. Identity relies on the fact that the seen situation becomes a reality in its entirety. That's means, that you see the situation from your relative future. Here is what happened, that you were at the right time, at the right place and in the right situation. Such inner messages need to be written with all possible details, because they can be very helpful tool on your way to your success. On other side, the analogies are principle of similarity. Similarity is an imaginary bridge between what you see in your current physical reality and what is in your inner reality. Therefore, the analogies are very important tool, which you have to know, to master and to use.

The whole concept of inspiration comes from within and is everywhere you are. Therefore, the inspiration is something so amazing that with it you can immediately become aware of your limitlessness.

Once you know it and once you have made your personal experience with imagination and inspiration, you are going to use the power of intuition.

Intuition is a generalizing moment in the time and space that gives you the opportunity to be an observer. Intuition is the universal language of success, the universal language of your life itself. All that intuition requires is your taking the situations as they are.

Example: At a specific time in the space, there are situations which as if they were dragging or moving you in a different direction, as your intellect do. At this moment in the space, you seem to have the choice to decide in which direction you can go. But that's not the case. You already predestined which situation you choose. This predestination was based on your assumed and accepted beliefs. The only thing that prevented you from choosing the intuition needs was your fear. The fear, that has been so deeply rooted in you and so long in the space feeded by its repetitions, that it has passed into a predestined decision. Such a decision was in complete contradiction or paradox with your nature, with your own life. This was the seed of all the unpleasant situations or failures.

As you can see, you have still the opportunity to change it. How? In the moment of decision. You have the possibility to feel it in the current moment and when you can feel it, you can also change it. The key is in your hands and the key has concrete name – decide for intuition.

Intuition is the only objectivity that you own. Anyone who is able to act immediately according to their intuition becomes an omniscient. That's not a joke, that's a fact. Just have your actions based on the unexpected, because that is the only real intuitive action.

Exercise one for developing an intuition:
This exercise is about re-establishment of intuitive well-being. It is a simple and progressive process that requires your peace and patience.

Start with one simple question in a day. Next questions add in terms of your progress. Just every time put yourself in relaxing mode, in your own way and ask.

Important to know – you can use your own questions of course.

1. What kind of feeling do I look for?
2. What is it what I wish for right now?
3. What is it what I need right now?
4. What I want to achieve at this moment?
5. What is my greatest talent at this moment?
6. What is my life goal?
7. With which area of my life am I most satisfied at this moment?
8. Do I want to achieve what I want?
9. How do I want achieve victory?
10. What I was afraid of most?
11. What was my biggest obstacle to succeed?
12. What kind of knowledge is it for me in this beautiful moment?

Exercise two for developing an intuition:
This exercise is about remembering and predestinating. It is a useful possibility, how to see the reality of your chosen situations. The main theme is to be aware of what you do to achieve your success.

Put yourself in peace in your own way. Let somebody read for you the following 22 questions and answer them as quickly as possible. Just be serious to yourself.

1. Male name?
2. Female name?
3. Gender?
4. Place?
5. Time?
6. Name of river?
7. Cardinal direction?
8. Animal?
9. Daytime (24-hour period)?
10. Sound?
11. Color?
12. Food?
13. Medicine?
14. Obstacle?
15. Weapon?
16. Fear?
17. Element?
18. Wish?
19. Memory?
20. Answer?
21. Solution?
22. Generalization?

After a year, return to them and you will be amazed of their depths. During my practice, I often see how this kind of exercise can help in various life situations. You can use also following statement to strengthen this exercise:

"I am the full and complete compassion of absolute that manifests in whole existence."

Once you know it and once you have made your personal experience with imagination, inspiration and intuition, you are going to use the power of visualization.

Visualization is often confused for imagination, what is a dangerous mistake and the reason why many people can't create what they sincerely wish for. Visualization is detail oriented action, while imagination is absolutely free from intellectual details. You can use the visualization until it is comfortable you for. This means that if thinking about the details causes you discomfort, stop with it immediately.

There are many teachings, which teach you about how you must visualize. There are many methods of visualization. You should be prudent, because each author gives you only his personal experience acquired through his personal experience. How it is possible to orientate in this huge tangle of information values? Which kind of visualization is better? From a sincere point of view, I have to say you – neither. Personal visualization allows you to step-by-step activate your own nature. Using active and guided visualization, it also stimulates your willpower and desire. Joyfulness is a major focus of all visualization techniques. By activating your own nature, you immediately overcome your sense of being "standard". Your nature is to be constantly in freedom, joyfulness, satisfaction, patience, concentration, understanding and action. The biggest mistake by practicing visualization is satisfaction with temporary relief from stress, temporary increase in standard daily abilities, or only increased visualization sensitivity. But, is it really so bad? No. It is just one of endless possibilities, how to increase your visualization skills. For better understanding and visualizing of this text, I introduce you a duality comparing – *Visualization assessment of the situation* (VAS) and *Intellectual assessment of the situation* (IAS).

$$Freedom\ (F) = \frac{\text{VAS}}{\text{IAS}}$$

$$F = \frac{\text{Emptiness}}{\text{Mindfulness}}$$

$$F = \frac{\text{Activate flowing thinking}}{\text{Activate rigid thinking}}$$

$$F = \frac{\text{Activate transformation of the energies and thoughts}}{\text{Activate observing of the energies and thoughts}}$$

$$F = \frac{\text{Activate observation what can be}}{\text{Activate constant observation of the unpleasant situation}}$$

$$F = \frac{\text{Activate orientation for joyfulness and satisfaction}}{\text{Activate orientation for stress and unpleasantness}}$$

$$F = \frac{\text{Activate actions beyond logic}}{\text{Activate logical actions}}$$

$$F = \frac{\text{Activate learning to know}}{\text{Activate easy vs. hard learning for learning}}$$

$$F = \frac{\text{Activate neurological sympathetic system}}{\text{Activate neurological parasympathetic system}}$$

As you can see, the correct-oriented visualization can lead to your wanted and desired results. The very power of visualization is working with all your senses and actions beyond whole ordinary experience.

Powerful visualization have its own steps.

1. Know what you want

It is essential to know what you want and you need to be able to imagine what you really want. Clarifying exactly what you want in your daily life, can be for someone a really hard job. Stop thinking such kind of thoughts which include negations to yourself, negations with which you have unknowingly robbed yourself. Such of thinking could be:

- I don't care.
- I don't want it.
- That doesn't really concern me.
- I am not interested.
- I'm not able to do it.
- I don't know what to do.
- I'll never stop caring.
- and so on.

You can look at from also in a different point of view. If you know what you don´t want, you automatically know what you want. That's simple. Another way to know what you want, or to strengthen what you want, is to look and search similar situations to what you want.

If you don't know what you want, you can use following statement (as often as you want) to know it:

"What is it, what I want right now?"

Hand in hand, there is necessary to make order in your past thinking structure. Our mind is programmed to work better, when forced to look for answers. The following questions will help you better understand what you really want:

- What's my ideal life description?
- What's my greatest superpower?
- What do I want to experience?
- What do I want to accomplish?
- What do I want to learn?
- Who do I want to be?
- Who do I want to be with?
- Where I want to be?

As a confirmation and strengthening of described "know what you want" process, I often recommend my clients and friends to use the following statement:

"I am in harmony with all that what I want."

Just keep in your mind what you want and always choose the way of the highest harmony with yourself.

2. Set the goal with clarity

Conscious clarity is to perceive any situation through your inner intelligence which is essence or your consciousness. There are two main types of clarity – *objective clarity* and *subjective clarity*. Objective clarity is directed with consciousness, while subjective clarity with social prejudices. You have to use, of course, the objective clarity, because with its power you can see the things as they are.

In order to know how to use the objective clarity, there are some important steps you have to handle. Your mind and heart must be in a harmonious dance of joy, therefore:

- Transform (interconnect) your mind into a tool of your heart.
- Think simply.
- Think with your heart.
- Allow the illuminated wisdom of your heart flow into your mind.

The illuminated wisdom of your heart is always with you. You can absolutely trust it. In the moment of absolute and unconditional trust in the illuminated wisdom or love of your heart, you have enabled it to leapfrog or connect with your mind. This connection brings you a huge contribution to your life. When I talk about transformation or interconnection of your mind into a tool of your heart, I mean exactly this process. When I talk about simple thinking and about thinking with your heart, I talk about process how to handle it. You have to be grateful for your heart feelings and you have to follow them in the best way you can.

After you already know about clarity, set your goal with this new and rejuvenating feeling.

Goal setting is a valuable skill, because it is a part of the predestination process. It involves envisioning a relative future outcome in your daily life, concrete timing, applying execution method and action to achieve it. Goals setting can help you make from your current place in the world a better or effective place, where you can show and use your full potential. At this place, do not forget the fundamental difference between the goal settings and the intention. Goal settings is a possibility to transform relativity of time and space (possibility to change the place or situation where you are), while intention is a transformation of your whole life.

Goals can give you more direction to your daily life and as you already know, our mind is programmed to work better, when forced to look for answers. Therefore, on the beginning of the goal setting process, you can ask yourself three following essential questions:

"Am I going to reach the goal?"

"Am I free and joyful with that goal?"

"What's next?"

While getting answers to the questions, you already started the automatic search process of your goals. Everything is happening at the same time and without delay. This applies to all themes of this book! So what's going on with your mind while setting goals? When you set goals, you are more focused on the situation you really want, because your mind was distracted to that moment. Setting of the goal or goals is a targeting to the current concreteness of your requirements. Targeting to the current concreteness is possible in many ways and following structure will for sure help you better targeting your required goals.

- Make difference between an idea and a goal. The difference between them is very simple. For an idea there is communication in the meaning of "I would like" or "I want", while by setting a goal, there is communication in the meaning of "I will" or "I have".
- Collecting goals make big sense. With writing all your possible goals in the current moment, you can see them as they are. Their classification and selection is clearly visible in this way, because they are now written and visible.
- Look for your priority No1 and set it as your *Big Bang Goal* (BBG) immediately.
- Select important areas of your BBG. These important areas may be personal development and stimulation, relationships, health, finance, career, education or all other possible areas. Never limit yourself, just write it.

- Select connections of all areas. These connections may be for example by the business area, the choosing of cooperation with existing companies, employment, self-employment, etc., or by the education area, the online learning, standard learning, personal training, etc.
- Use more detail if they are needed and comfortable. With using of more details you can go the very depth of your goal. For example by the business area, with choosing of self-employment, you can look for more details with questioning as "What kind of self-employment?" or "Which area of self-employment" or "Which place of self-employment", etc. Just use your body and the space you live in current moment.

In order for you to define your goal successfully and clearly, you must confirm the previous structure in some way in your mind. Use the following three steps as an absolutely confirmation of your goal.

- Use the power of focus on concentration, because that accumulates everything you know to this point and results in the arising of cleaner kind of knowing what you want.
- Realize immediately your nature. This means, you shouldn't make a differentiation of yourself and others. The sense of that statement is, that you should be open

for any opportunity, which is coming. Just go beyond your mental social ideas.
- Actualize the information values in your daily life. How to do it or practice it? There shouldn't be a difference between what you think and what you do. Have in mind that everything you think and do, becomes an expression of realization. Actualization makes you know, that everything is good as it is.

There is one big question I often heard not only from my clients and friends. The question was "If there are so many instructions on how to be successful, why don't they work for everybody?" Most of them has set their goals in a bad emotional mood. They set their goals out of a state of unpleasantness and from lack of something concrete or not-concrete. To such kind of action I immediately say "Stop doing it". Never, I repeat, never ever set goals out of a lack and from the need to compare something. Such kind of success creating does not work and is counterproductive. That's exactly one of the reasons why I wrote this and other books. You need to see a wider context, not just what is presented to you as your everyday reality. That's not your reality, it is a temporary social response to what you have done in the past days. You cannot compare to something that no longer exists. Deal with who you really are in your beautiful body and change your reality in the way you want. Just be patient and attentive, the answers are in you and around you. You are a creator, not a slave.

3. Set the method

There is no bad method, there is only different approach and handling with methods. I recommend you following exercise structure for your visualization skills, which begins with a powerful statement:

"I acknowledge and honor this situation, thereby purify it."

- Look and search inside, which means, you should go into your mind where you either remember or create new images.
- Observe the images and analyze them into their last detail. Be patient, precious and breathe peacefully.
- Hold the images as strong as you can and as long as is comfortable with using all your mental power.

This type of exercise is designed to achieve better visualization capabilities. If you're just starting your visualization practice but aren't quite sure how to go about it, it's absolutely all right. Be easy to take a break, or go to do any other activity, or just relax. Hastiness and impatience has not helped anyone yet to achieve the desired effect.

Athletes in my gym often say "When he could prove it, I can do it as well." They saw success, they visualized success by transforming for their current needs and they achieved success. So simple is the process of "set the method" principle which I wrote about.

4. Be joyful

Visualization must be practiced with joy. It is important to avoid any necessity in your practice and in your daily life. Searching, feeling and seeing joy is the next key to achieving everything you want.

The following structure is a possibility to leave an unpleasant situation immediately.

- *Don't change the situation, change the strategy of your way you react to the situation*

Example: Most of this population use a huge amount of their energy to change the unpleasant situation in a miraculous and instantaneous way. At the same time, they wonder, that they are not feeling well. This is logical when the most valuable thing, their energy potential, has passed in the opposite direction. There is a simple solution here. One have to react peaceful in any situation. This is the changing strategy No1.

- *Change your communication skills*

Example: If you look around, you will find out how many unnecessary words are constantly manifested. All this is wasting a rare energy potential of the well-being. Instead of saying "something terrible happened", you can say "there was a change" or instead of saying "I am not doing well", you can say "I made big changes to my well-being", or instead of saying "I do not know what to do" you can say "I'm in the state of receiving great ideas" and so on. Just see the situations from other angle of view.

- *Look on the bright side*

Example: Look at the ten people you know they are not satisfied about what they have. What feelings you have by observing them? Now, look at the ten people you know they are absolutely satisfied about what they have. What feelings you have by observing these happy people?

It is necessary and desirable that you devote yourself to the things that make you happy. As you already know, success is subordinate to certain laws, including the particular the law of similarity. Just look on the bright side.

To be joyful is to be in harmony with yourself, therefore make every day to be your joyful day. Here are some small tips to make your day better than it was:

- Wake up with a smile
- Take a breakfast
- Be grateful that you woke up today
- Breathe easily
- Read new books
- Listen new music
- Learn something new
- Do something unexpected, go behind your habits
- Take a break from seriousness
- Meditate

There are countless ways to make your day happier. Just move in the direction of joy.

5. Create a vision board

Vision board ideas are many times a useful tool for better visualization. It is very inspirational to see, what you want. You can use the system from the "set the goal with clarity" and make from it a vision board, or you make it in another way. Just make your own. It's absolutely on you, because it's your own interpersonal way you are.

Whether you place it on your wall or on your night stand, the vision board serves you as a reminder to live each day to its fullest potential while continually striving towards understanding for others as well as yourself. Vision board reminds you of what you really want from your heart.

One of the so called "secret keys" to success is to focus on situations you desire, not to situations you fear. I have some ideas for you from my life experience, how to make a powerful vision board. Just be creative and do it as a joyful play. Use them in the best way:

- *Use blank platform*

Blank platform allows you to be a creator in the current time. It's a huge impulse for your subconscious and even consciousness. They know now, that you are the creator.

- *Use colors*

For your highest comfort, use the full range of colors and use one color extra, which you've never used.

- *Use geometric shapes*

Using geometric shapes allows you to see your current harmony. This is very powerful tool.

- *Use labyrinth*

This tool is the gateway to yourself. Labyrinth can leave only the strongest and you are the strongest.

- *Use slogans*

Slogans are a motivating tool that transforms itself, so it needs to be continually changed and complemented.

- *Use all kinds of photos*

Using different photos is a good starting visualization tool. It's a direct enrichment of your imagination, but keep in mind that someone already owns it. Don´t put yourself in the role of a slave, but stay in a role of a joyful observer of your happiness and success.

- *You have time*

Work on your vision board daily and don't let your self be overwhelmed of the time limitations.

- *Put your final product in decorative frame*

In this way you confirm the seriousness of the whole process of creating your vision board.

The previous structure will definitely help you and I recommend you a 22-day process of creating your own form of vision board. Why 22-day and not 21 or 30? I really like to work with combinations of numbers in my life and also in my practice. The 22-day process of creating has proven itself in my life experience and is extremely popular among my clients and friends. For that reason, I am presenting you one such a 22-day technique to create your own form of vision board.

ay one

Main theme of the day

The power of knowing

What to use

On the first day use your current knowing, skills, self-confidence and your active life formation. This means that you have accumulated all your experience to this current point in the time and space. Leave all your worries about what you do not know yet or what you would like to know or have, just be proud of what you know right now.

Write answers to the following questions
(Describe the situations and your feelings)

Have you ever tried to manipulate others?
What was your best action until today?
What was the best result of your creative thinking until today?
What was your best skill until today?
Today's experience?

Day two

Main theme of the day
The secret truths

What to use

*Use your unconscious power, your sixth sense and your
clarity. That means, that in order to be back in harmony,
you have to use the expression of patience, understanding, consideration and all the good deeds. You should be
a manifested helper, healer and teacher, or better to say,
someone who use the nature powers for the well-being.*

Write answers to the following questions
(Describe the situations and your feelings)

*Have you ever been vengeful, affectional, with wrong
judgment, or just passive without interest?
When you were intuitive until today and what an experience was it for you?
Have you ever been able to help or counsel someone with
absolutely amazing result?
In which situation did you get the most out of your patience?
Today's experience?*

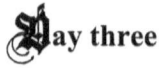ay three

Main theme of the day
The inexhaustible source

What to use
Use your vividness, mental fertility, growth and the possibility to create a new life (you create new life in every moment). At the physical level, is it using of your beautiful body. At the internal level are all the wise ideas, abundance of discoveries and knowledge.

Write answers to the following questions
(Describe the situations and your feelings)

Have you ever been vanity, superficial, unfaithful, unable to deal with situations, or have you chosen your partner for profitability?
Have you ever experienced wealth and fertility?
When were you able to create something?
What did you do the best for your health or well-being?
Today's experience?

Day four

Main theme of the day

Creating a structure

What to use

Use your structure of willpower and desire for stability, safety and durability. This is your effort for independence from the limitations of the social system, from its unpredictability. On this day be attentive on the sense of order, discipline and responsibility to handle or to make a better business. Just don't be stiff.

Write answers to the following questions
(Describe the situations and your feelings)

Have you ever enforce your own interests at the expense of someone else?
Have you ever experienced independence?
Have you ever been able to make a better business than ever before?
When did you feel absolutely safe?
Today's experience?

 **ay five**

Main theme of the day
The world of faith

What to use

Use your comprehension, because through that you can strengthen your self-confidence and self-reliance. This is the favorable alignment of situations process. Also, you are in a position to do your personal intentions that result from your essential and natural values. On this day, you faced the world of faith and a deep faith based on sincere confession.

Write answers to the following questions
(Describe the situations and your feelings)

Have you ever provided someone with intentional wrong advice?

Have you ever given someone a perfect advice to get what he/she wanted?

Have you ever provided to someone a good terms for co-operation?

Have you ever provided someone with spiritual help?

Today's experience?

Day six

Main theme of the day

The world of decisiveness

What to use

Use your love to yourself. Let out your past habits and with honor affirm your current decisiveness. This is the point of important decisions that are free from duality. Today is the day, when you should decide with your heart.

Write answers to the following questions
(Describe the situations and your feelings)

Where did you meet the biggest disappointment?
Have you ever made a great decision?
Have you ever experienced honest and enriching cooper-ation?
Have you ever experience a sincere and enriching love?
Today's experience?

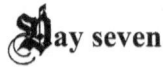

Day seven

Main theme of the day
Moving forward

What to use
Use your ambitions, searching for new possibilities, or simply the desire to have a value. Today, you leave a well-known way (habits) and go out on your own journey. Today is the "D-day". This is a decision, daring desire and willing to take the path forward. Focus today on one area that you do not understand well (not for an enormous life situation) and use your skills to get out of it with a profit (mental or physical).

Write answers to the following questions
(Describe the situations and your feelings)

Have you ever experience personal or business defeat or failure?
When did you overcome the obstacle/-s successfully?
When did you move forward and you were amazed by the correctness of this decision?
When did you felt your highest value?
Today's experience?

Day eight

Main theme of the day

The best organization

What to use

Use your sense for detail, clarity, objectivity, decisive judgment and honesty. Let this day be a highlight a high level of responsibility for your action. You have to observe today the duality of reactions. If you did something, what did you get for it? Be honest, truthful and responsible and watch the amazing situations happening around you.

Write answers to the following questions
(Describe the situations and your feelings)

Have you ever been unfair or you had a trouble with the law?
Have you ever been in the role of justice?
What was the best result of your decision?
When did you felt to be in highest harmony?
Today's experience?

ay nine

Main theme of the day
Soothing pause

What to use
Use your past life phase in which you defended your-selves, to get out of your current experience. Today is an important experience in which you can find out who you are, what you want and where are you going. Take a look at the depth of your daily life situations and the level of awareness how your actions are.

Write answers to the following questions
(Describe the situations and your feelings)
When did you feel the greatest loneliness and abandon-ment?
Have you ever reevaluated your thoughts about yourself and the world?
Have you ever experienced success in education?
Have you ever had an interest in spiritual teachings?
Today's experience?

ay ten

Main theme of the day

The world of happiness

What to use

Use your existing power due to which you everyday wake up and thanks to which you can continually grow and advance. This power is in depth of all situations you thought you had no influence on them. You had simply justified your failures with weather, traffic situation, social systems, or the intervention of some "higher power". Today, take a look at situations you have previously been justifying in some way.

Write answers to the following questions
(Describe the situations and your feelings)

Have you ever felt disfavor of fate?
Have you ever experienced the intervention of fate in a good direction?
Have you ever experienced a new and better opportunity?
When did you feel your greatest power?
Today's experience?

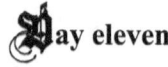

Day eleven

Main theme of the day

The secret of the inner power

What to use

Use your kindness and gentle action. Today is your day of balance between conscious and unconscious. This day emphasizes that your goal should not be to hide your instinctive nature. You should hide your old habits. Open the enormous power of yourself which you can use through your kindness and gentle action.
Today, watch and enjoy your pleasure, kindness and gentle action.

Write answers to the following questions
(Describe the situations and your feelings)

Have you ever abused your power?
Have you ever experienced the power of will?
Have you ever experienced courage?
When did you felt your greatest physical strength?
Today's experience?

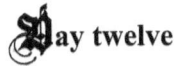ay twelve

Main theme of the day
The new angle of view

What to use

Use your passivity as if it was your greatest skill. Today is your big day of changing the angle of view. Nothing will be more like what it seemed to be. External stiffness can also be seen as an opportunity to reach a change of needed new angle of view and a change of life through peaceful behavior.
Choose today one simple situation (for example coffee drinking) that you have previously seen in the same way. Now, look at this situation from a completely different angle of view.

Write answers to the following questions
(Describe the situations and your feelings)

Have you ever been stagnant?
Have you ever turned or changed your values?
Have you ever observed the world in a different way?
When did you feel your greatest changing possibility?
Today's experience?

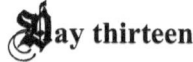
ay thirteen

Main theme of the day
The greatest liberation

What to use

Use all the finished situations you have in mind, but also those that you can no longer remember. Use all the great power of them for your new beginning. The greatest liberation is end of one piece of your life and at the same time the beginning of something new and better. The end does not mean something bad. Take a look at today's situation (again something simple), which is already finished. Think about what positive the situation has brought to you.

Write answers to the following questions
(Describe the situations and your feelings)

Have you ever experienced some painful farewells?
Have you ever experienced situation that ended with your disappointed feeling, but later it turned out that it was a positive change?
When did you finish something with a good feeling?
When did you feel your greatest liberation?
Today's experience?

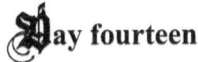ay fourteen

Main theme of the day

Gentleness of thinking, talking and acting

What to use

Use your hope and confidence. Today is full of hope and therefore you have to treat yourself with respect and admiration. Taste the fruits of your thinking, talking and acting, you have manifested as a hope. There is always hope for better-felt life situations.
Take them all.

Write answers to the following questions
(Describe the situations and your feelings)

Have you ever crossed the level of generally accepted normality?
Have you ever experienced a gradual change?
Did you ever experience unexpected, but in the same time well-felt healing?
When did you feel your gentleness?
Today's experience?

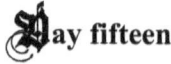

Day fifteen

Main theme of the day

The world of opposites

What to use

Use your knowing about duality. You already know, that what is good for you, don't need to be good for me. We all have our own face of life. Today, note all the nice and tempting offers. It can be anything around you. Everything you observe with your senses is offered to you and you can handle it as you want.

Write answers to the following questions
(Describe the situations and your feelings)

Have you ever let someone manipulate or control you?
Have you ever been aware of your contradictory sites?
Have you ever experienced situations where only good offers have ever came to you?
When did you (most) think about good and bad?
Today's experience?

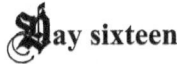

Day sixteen

Main theme of the day

Structure and dimension of the life security

What to use

Use your certainty, that you have acquired through your life experiences. Structure and dimension of your life security depends on certainty that should be unquestionable. For this reason, you must get rid of your convictions and prejudices. Today, be aware of situations you are thinking about, that they are your biggest certainty.

Write answers to the following questions
(Describe the situations and your feelings)

Have you ever experienced any situations that didn't go according to your imagine?
Have you ever experienced a surprising positive situation?
Have you ever had a really quick idea or solution?
When did you feel absolutely secure?
Today's experience?

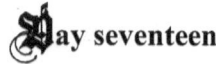 **ay seventeen**

Main theme of the day
Look into higher contexts

What to use
Use your strategic ability and add more structure to your written and verbal communication. Today, show that you are starting or planning for situations that you will achieve in the future and to which you can put your rightful hopes.

Write answers to the following questions
(Describe the situations and your feelings)

Have you ever feel "out from reality"?
Have you ever experienced the fulfillment of your wishes?
Have you ever planned something that made a successful result during this planning?
Have you ever feel as you got an answer for everything?
Today's experience?

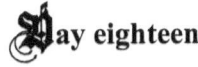 **ay eighteen**

Main theme of the day
The world of vision

What to use

Use your anticipations, desires, dreams, fantasy and overall perception. All this is the entrance to your inner world of visions. Take some time today (10 minutes are enough), when you are only dreaming about the various situations. After that, let it act and just observe it.

Write answers to the following questions
(Describe the situations and your feelings)

Have you ever been afraid of the darkness or the de-mons?
Has something ever helped you what you couldn't explain at all?
Have you ever had an inspirational dreams?
What was your greatest inspiration?
Today's experience?

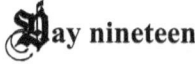ay nineteen

Main theme of the day
Joy of life

What to use

Use your vitality, euphoria and optimism. These are the three co-workers of consciousness with which you achieve inner purity and overcome all worries, irritations and fear. Observe and active search happiness and joy around you today. Feel all the freedom behind them.

Write answers to the following questions
(Describe the situations and your feelings)

Have you ever been too much active or destructive?
What does youthful freshness mean for you?
How would you characterize the sunny side of life?
What was your greatest joy?
Today's experience?

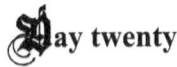ay twenty

Main theme of the day

Your intention is your treasure

What to use

Use your positive judging skills. Today, you are taking a decisive step in gaining self-worth, in which you change negativity into positiveness. This is a form of liberation from worries and problems, from unpleasant situations and commitments, from obstacles and fears. Therefore, focus today on your daily intentions and feel whole the beautiful freedom in them.

Write answers to the following questions
(Describe the situations and your feelings)

Have you ever done a thoughtless act with negative con-
sequences?
How would you describe the birth?
Have you ever experienced the fulfillment of your goals?
What does the treasure mean to you?
Today's experience?

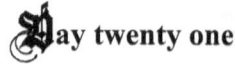

Day twenty one

Main theme of the day
Rediscovering the unity

What to use

*Use everything you see in you and around you. Use all
that pictures and make them be one. You are the result of
some concrete development that is within you and all
around you. Look for a "happy ends" today and enjoy it.
In the "happy ends" is the ability to fulfill your goals.
Answers are everywhere. You have already made a significant and decisive step in understanding your value, in
true authenticity and integrity.*

Write answers to the following questions
(Describe the situations and your feelings)

*Have you ever been in the state that you have not com-
pleted or finished something?
How would you describe the unity?
Have you ever been at the right time, in the right place
and with the right people?
What does the fulfillment mean to you?
Today's experience?*

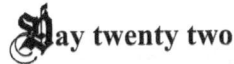 **ay twenty two**

Main theme of the day
Return

What to use

Use your faithfulness, talent, perfection and ability to successfully start and finished situations. The ability to create new structures and to finish the old structures is the art you carry in yourself. Today observe the situations you start and finish (this are all kind of situations as the simplest one - open and closing the door or breathing). Just watch them how they are coming and going.

Write answers to the following questions
(Describe the situations and your feelings)

Have you ever been dependent on someone or something?
How would you describe new beginning?
Have you ever felt your nature so strong that you were convinced that you can have what you want and be what you want?
What could be the living symbol of yourself?
Today's experience?

6. Relax

Relaxation is a form of reducing mental and physical tension. There is no need to look for some extra science. The relaxation is in fact an action which is free from the tension of duality. That's mean, in the state of relaxation you are active as never before and that's the ground why have the relaxation so wondrous effect on your mental and physical health. If you are able to relax, your all actions arise spontaneously from the non-dual state.

Relaxation is a direct input into the factory of mind, so pay close attention to it. Relax always according to yourself, because only you know what the relaxation mean for you and how to get there. Here are some steps to keep in mind:

- *Understand stress and relaxation*

The most important thing you need to know about relaxation is that it is a stressful situation. Yes, you read well, it's a stressor. About stress there are written billions of articles, but the so-called stress hides a great momentum. All that is outside of your adopted behavior (all your habits) is by itself taken as a stressful effect. It is simply a violation of the concept in order to establish a next, better concept. At this moment of decision occurs, what kind of stressful reaction is going to happen. That's why I constantly emphasize the importance of looking at situations from a different perspective. Each moment is a stressor and it's up to you how you handle it.

- *Change what you see and feel for something completely different*

If you were in a situation where you could not relax enough, it meant you tried too hard to be relaxed. In such of moment it is enough to change the strategy of your habits and do something unexpected. For example, take a cake, or make with someone an independent conversation, or listen to the music, or anything else where you can no more think about what you wanted before.

- *Breathe*

Already with just something as simple and natural as the focus on your breathing, you have entered a state of relaxation.

- *Adhere personal discipline*

Do not let yourself be neglected for so long until it brings you into an uncomfortable mental state. Learn regularity, then make regularity unnecessary and then the unnecessarity turn to joy.

This is the game where we divide ourselves into two poles – the good and the bad. This is the trap of 'need to be relaxed as reference point'. You don't need to do nothing, you only can do whatever you want. Don´t be bewildered by someone else's habits. Relaxation is more a question of the freedom to accept someone else's habits and the freedom to trust the essential goodness of yourselves and the others.

7. Move it in your present reality

As you already know, it is essential to communicate in the present time. Your visualization should therefore be transformed into your current moment (as if already is) and not to a relative future. Moving your visualization into the present reality is simple. It have its own rules, as follow:

- *Importance of current moment*

Each moment contains cycles of birth and death, therefore at any moment you have the opportunity to adjust or completely change your reality.

- *Perception of current moment*

Willpower, desire and the mind are the factors, you have to work with. Let them cooperate by avoiding of the negative thoughts, words and actions (ignorance, anger, envy, pride, overall abuses, etc.).

- *Knowledge of current moment*

Recognize that you are and you know the current moment. It can help following statement:

"I know this is my amazing and beautiful body, thanks to which I am expressing here."

- *Illusion of current moment*

Every moment you are in the moment. Where else would you like to be? Think about it!

- *Awaking from current moment*

Learn through traditional practice, symbolism and philosophy. It helps you to understand everything.

8. Use comfortable details

As I have earlier mentioned, dealing with details has to be particularly comfortable. When working with the details, I recommend the following system.

- Understand the basic components
- Identify the path of the important components
- Consider three parameters: *1. Positive, negative, neutral; 2. Its similarity; 3. The force acting upon the components by the law of similarity;*
- Put all components together to build a comprehensible structure
- Practice "base-pairing" of components with comprehensible examples
- Check it one more time with a distance
- Focus and memorizing the important components

9. Be specific

Once you've completed the entire process, make it as one and the exact product. The specification is extremely important not only for visualization techniques but also for whole communication. To be specific means to use your own facts, details and feelings to make sure you are communicating absolutely clearly. You have to know, that also specificity is relative, therefore is this process only visible for your interpersonal understanding.

10. Repeat

When your old habits returns, when they are reincorporated in your daily activities, everything occurs again as it has before, but what's more, with greater intensity (the relative good and bad consequences). This is exactly how it works also with repeating your visualization. But if you've followed all the steps necessary to create a powerful visualization, you've won the jackpot.

The law of repeating is astonishing. There are many people always repeat their same dramas. What I'm going to reveal to you will probably surprise you. Do you know the meaning of the word "repetition"? Repetition is interpreted as a particular act that is performed more than once. But that is not quite true. In terms of relativity in order to achieve expected success, the meaning of the word "repetition" is directed to a disposable act in the current time and space. This disposable act can be of course strengthened by its repetition. But if you make your visualization perfect for the first time, no repetition is necessary. How do you know that your visualization was done perfectly for the first time? By seeing immediate positive changes in your life, towards your expected success.

If "repetition" is interpreted as a particular act that is performed more than once, you have to know, that such a description only applies to the dual system and is used to control individuals and crowds. Think for a moment. If a company wanted to sell a product, it must necessarily create a requirement in the social system by repeatedly submitting information about the product. All the manipulation (positive and also negative) works in this system, in the law of repetition. Repetition in the sense of social communication is an absolutely undesirable and destructive act.

If you need to repeat your visualization, act with absolute knowing on why you intend to do so. There is nothing worse than thinking that you are doing the right thing. You have to know and not to think that you know. Visualization is only difficult for those with restlessness minds. Be in peace, do not hurry for something just because it offers the system around you.

It is indisputable that certain practices need to be repeated in the exact number. It has its deep mathematical and philosophical reason. The mathematical number of repeats is directly related to the physical world that is transformed in this way, but that's absolutely another theme. You have to know, that visualization is a disposable act and its possible repetition must be done with the awareness of why it is repeated. All your action needs to be as comfortable and natural as possible with its simplicity. You can use following statement:

"All the accomplishments are obtained through the power of my thinking and their repetition. Let them be an enrichment for myself and all beings!"

The previous steps I've offered you are powerful tools to make your visualization strong as possible.

Each of us has its own practice and rituals, but all of them are beneficial only to our own visualization practice. Follow only your own practice, because exactly that practice suits best to your own preferences. There are no strict requirements for visualization practice and rituals, as mind is the main focus of such kind of practicing. In the social system, however, you are required to follow clearly defined, step-by-step exercises, rituals and many others practices established by coaches, trainers, speakers, teachers, etc. You can follow all the visualization systems if you wish and if it is comfortable for you. Of course, it is more desirable if you receive empowerment inside of you before you start visualization practice.

Before you start, just be in comfortable posture. You can sit, you can stay, or you can lie down. Do it your way. Leave all thoughts about yourself behind and have no worry about your health, money, relationships, learning, personal development, etc.

In order to become connected with your visualization, you must cultivate your thinking. Just let your thoughts be the thoughts and stay in the undisturbed state of observer. You can use following statement:

"I am doing this visualization for the joyfulness of myself and all beings."

Once you know it and once you have made it to your personal experience with imagination, inspiration, intuition and visualization, you are going to use the power of renunciation.

"Renunciation the need to receive, replace it for the opportunity to give and revenue what you have renounced."

This is exactly the first thing, what I tell to all, who are beyond the point of visualization. This is an interested moment in which "breaks the bread", whether you will or can be successful or not.

Renunciation the need to receive is at this moment a confirmation of confidence in achieving the desired success. When you study the philosophy of "how to be there where I want to be", you often hear this word "renunciation". Maybe you, as many others, thought it means you have to stop eat too much, stop abuse drugs, stop drinking alcohol, stop smoking, or something else. Others thinks it is some way of abandoning your current life and taking the life of the ascetic. This is all a mistake of identical understanding. Your ideas have nothing to do with this very interesting process of renunciation. Renunciation, in this sense, is only one part of the whole confirmation process.

About the "renunciation the need to receive" you have to know, that you are complete. There is nothing to be done. You've already done everything. Now you just have to enjoy it, you have to enjoy all the fruit of your work.

If you would constantly addressing the demands of your relative future success (for example with visualization), as I have already mentioned a few times, you would only revive your perceived lack of success. This is not the way you should use it. Use only the way of confirmation joy. How to practice the renunciation? Here are some helpful strategy steps for you:

- *Don't grasp social happiness and pleasure at all*
What a powerful and ambiguous statement. Failure to understand the relative quality of temporary social pleasures causes you to be in unpleasant situation. You have to recognize between the assumed requirements (external naturalized social goals) and your personal requirements (your own goals). Therefore, happiness and pleasure must come from your inside, it must be your own uniqueness.
- *Experience pleasure while remaining detached*
Many are disturbed when they hear about giving up of ownership. They think, that they must suffer in order to achieve some kind of inner peace, harmony, liberation, or something else what they don't understand and what they don't have an experience with. Your aim is to achieve a beautiful state beyond all suffering. You have to experience pleasure concentrating on the good things. Whatever has happened, it is necessary to focus on the better aspects of life. Focus on just one positive detail. This actively chosen activity attracts you more and more similar situations. That's your indescribable ability to transform.

-   Investigate and understand

For your own protection, it is essential to investigate and understand the real nature of your relative existence. Thus, in the sense to know the real nature of your relative existence, you must investigate and understand the relativity of your past actions.

Remember the three situations where you expected something nice, but instead of pleasure, you were disappointed. Also, remember the three situations where you expected disappointment, but instead disappointment came big and surprising pleasure.

The second way, how to investigate and understand the real nature of your relative existence, is reading the traditional scripture. This is my favorite way. The modern traditions has taken on innumerable forms throughout the centuries. There are many articles and lectures that explain the most famous and widely known world scriptures. You have to choose the best for you. I really enjoy to read the Sacred Hindu, Jain, White Tantric, Buddhist, Taoist, Confucian, Dervish, Gnostic, Judaism, Islamic, Alchemy, Christian and many other Texts.

The third way is to take instructions from teachers. Here I do not mean certified teachers or self-proclaimed gurus, but real teachers who provide you with a real treasures of knowing. These are exceptional personalities who give you undisputable information values. If you meet him, you know that it is him.

The fourth way are all other possible ways you can choose.

- *Do not expect a mystery*

There is no mystery and no secret at all. There are only interpersonal experiences, which are provided from the point where you are, to the points that are "as if" outside of you. How to understand it? You can easily understand it according to the law of coverage. One-point commercial is achievable for millions of potential recipients. That's it. If you accept some concrete information value, you are already started to handle it. To handle it means you multiply it. To multiply it means, you manipulate your space. To manipulate your space means, you change the space. You are a mystery to anyone who doesn't know you. Well, as soon as he knows you, the whole assumption of mystery has disappeared.

As you see now, mere giving up of objects from your reality will not help you. No matter what kind of practice you do, you should always act with honesty. As a confirmation, you can use following statement:

"Let it be beneficial to all beings."

Why is not in that statement "me and all beings?". Because there is no separation between you and others. The success of others is your success too. Generate this thought within yourself and you will see the greatness of your potential. Renunciation is a beautiful and important process. I have for you next 22 day system to strengthen renunciation.

ay one

Main theme of the day

The power of creative intelligence

What to use

*On the first day use your current creative intelligence.
This means that you have accumulated all your creative
experience to this current point in the time and space.
Leave all your worries about your creativity, just be
proud of what you have achieved so far.
Choose a regular activity you do automatically and make
from it something creative.*

Write answers to the following questions
(Describe the situations and your feelings)

*Have you ever failed in creativity?
What was your best creative day?
What was the best result of your creativity?
What does creativity mean to you?
Today's experience?*

ay two

Main theme of the day

The power of transparent intelligence

What to use

Use your communication skills, because this is the beginning of your inner communication in order to strengthen your renunciation. Your transparent intelligence is impersonal, universal and is beyond social personality, beyond the ego ("mine, mine, mine...").

Before you start communicating today, choose the way that is most appropriate in according to strengthen your renunciation.

Write answers to the following questions
(Describe the situations and your feelings)

Have you ever felt like being "dragged down"?
What everything is made by you?
If you could choose to specialize in your communication, what would it be and why?
In which situation did you get the most out of your communication?
Today's experience?

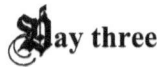

Day three

Main theme of the day

The power of unification of intelligence

What to use

Use all your negotiation skills, trade skills and public re-lations. Today is a day of unity. Unity in business sense is determined by the state of your business relations. This, of course, does not always mean success. Success comes at the moment of your unification of intelligence.
Choose two regular activities you do automatically and make from them one new activity.

Write answers to the following questions
(Describe the situations and your feelings)

Have you ever had a negative experience with business travel, general transportation, business closing, business negotiation or public relations?
Have you ever experienced unity between you and your partner?
When were you able to connect people or teams so that connection has led to success?
What did you do the best for your health or well-being? Today's experience?

Day four

Main theme of the day
The power of development

What to use

Use your understanding for situation and ability to transform it. Many did not realize they are capable to understand and transform all kinds of things and situations. Today you are entering the state of receiving a gift and therefore be aware of the elements which are present in everything around you.

Write answers to the following questions
(Describe the situations and your feelings)

Have you ever been in a situation where you have "not understand at all"?
Which three areas in world you understand and also know, you can transform it anytime you want?
Have you ever received an unexpected gift?
What means for you development?
Today's experience?

# Day five

Main theme of the day

The power of enabling perspective

What to use

Use your ability to see, to observe, reflect, contemplate, discern and positively judge. This day gives your life situations their properties.

Choose one simple situation in your daily life. Observe it for a while and look how important for you it is.

Write answers to the following questions
(Describe the situations and your feelings)

Have you ever lose something very valuable?
What kind of contemplation brings you most joy and satisficing?
From what perspective would you like to observe your life?
What's the highest value in your life?
Today's experience?

ay six

Main theme of the day

The power of communication

What to use

*Use your strength, fortress, hardness and flexibility. To-
day, there is an extraordinary opportunity to express the
power of communication – both, external and internal.
Begin this morning with exercise (any kind of exercise)
and observe the amazing unity behind it. Also observe the
positive impact of this exercise on your activity throughout the day.*

Write answers to the following questions
(Describe the situations and your feelings)

*Have you ever felt completely lonely and "lost"?
Have you ever experienced the beauty of the traditional
yogic or other traditional practices?
Have you ever felt the unity of your thoughts with what
you are talking about?
How would you unite the whole world and the universe?
Today's experience?*

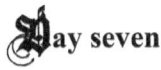ay seven

Main theme of the day
The power of dividing

What to use
*Use both your site – positively and negatively perceived.
Use your good perception, sharpness, precision, cleverness and resolving ability. Today you have the ability to
divide, which also means to differentiate and classify.
Take one situation that you considered as indivisible and
inseparable. Find ways to divide it and strengthen it at
the same time.*

Write answers to the following questions
(Describe the situations and your feelings)
*Have you ever experienced that you work only with your
"bad or negative site"?
When did your properties as the good perception, sharpness, precision, cleverness and resolving ability helped
you?
Have you ever divided something fairly so that all stake-
holders were happy and satisfied?
How would you divide this world and universe to make
everyone happy?
Today's experience?*

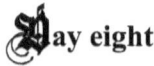ay eight

Main theme of the day
The power of space cultivation

What to use
Practice your current location, position and place. Today you will strengthen your ability to act from where you are, wherever it is.
Choose your standard daily location. Just be free and joyfully where you are, with thoughts on:
"I am the heart of this place".

Write answers to the following questions
(Describe the situations and your feelings)

Have you ever hated a place so much, that you have run from it or completely moved away?
What are the places that make you feel very happy and pleasant after you see them?
Have you ever cultivated some place (by design changing or something else)?
Which place is for you most powerful, where you feel absolutely free and full of creative power?
Today's experience?

ay nine

Main theme of the day
The power of regeneration

What to use
Use your wits, sophistication, experience, perseverance and patience. Regeneration is the most important way after completing any activity. Be grateful that something as amazing as the ability to regenerate is your natural possibility.

Choose three situations today, after that you relax. You can make just a simple stretching, with the awareness that it is a regeneration after the activity.

Write answers to the following questions
(Describe the situations and your feelings)
Have you ever felt so tired, that you were sick out of it? What kind of activity has relieved you rfom tension and stress?

Have you ever experienced meditation techniques? If a regeneration model existed, how would it look structural?

Today's experience?

Day ten

Main theme of the day

The power of your skills

What to use

*Use your analytical, conceptual, critical, deductive, com-
mercial awareness, confidence, adaptability and other
interpersonal and communication qualities. Today you
are aware of the tremendous endless possibilities which
are still in you.*

*Today, just keep an eye on the ease with which you are
doing what you have so far considered to be obvious.*

Write answers to the following questions
(Describe the situations and your feelings)

Have you ever thought you had any talent at all?
*What benefits are, that you know you have ability to do
something?*
Have you ever experienced moment of excellence?
*What did you decide alone for the last time? Describe 10
situations.*
Today's experience?

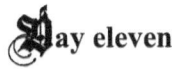

Day eleven

Main theme of the day
The power of comprehension

What to use
Use your adaptation to different situations and the ability to establish order. Today you are in the field of comprehension, what is one of your secret weapons to transform each situation.

Focus on three situations you understand. Think about what was the benefit for you.

Write answers to the following questions
(Describe the situations and your feelings)

Have you ever felt lost in understanding of certain situation?
Which area do you understand most?
Have you ever made the order (order in your own thoughts, order in the family, order at work, or just simply cleaning your room, etc.)?
What does comprehension mean to you?
Today's experience?

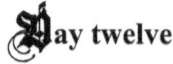

Day twelve

Main theme of the day
The power of right fuel

What to use

*Use your ability to breathe. Today you realize that the
ability to breathe is the driving force of creation.
Today, every hour stop doing what you do and observe
your breathing ability. Not the breathing alone, but the
ability to breathe, that means, what is behind your physiological breathing.*

Write answers to the following questions
(Describe the situations and your feelings)

*Have you ever had the feeling that you cannot breathe?
When did you felt comfortable filled and when comforta-
ble empty?
Have you ever experienced traditional breathing tech-
niques?
How would you create life?
Today's experience?*

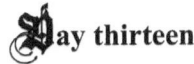

Day thirteen

Main theme of the day

The power of mirror

What to use

Use all external observed objects and also all internal observed objects. Today you understand that everything is the mirror of everything and that everything is positive influenced, positive complemented and positive enriched one another.

Choose one common situation and think about how it affects you and your loved ones or friends.

Write answers to the following questions
(Describe the situations and your feelings)

Have you ever made someone guilty of your failure or to the factors of the failure?

Have you ever identified yourself with someone else's behavior?

Have you ever become a perfect example for someone?

How would the mirror of your life look like?

Today's experience?

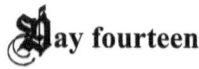
Day fourteen

Main theme of the day
The power of combining

What to use
Use all your physiological and mental senses. Today, you can see that combining is something absolutely natural. Combining is your naturalness that you performed unknowingly and automatically.
Focus on such a common thing as speech (also inner speaking). Think about the process that combines the final sentences.

Write answers to the following questions
(Describe the situations and your feelings)

Have you ever had a problem combining something?
If you can combine the words into sentences (also your inner mental speaking), what does it say about you?
If motion means change and if you can do just the smallest movements (also your inner mental movements), what does it say about you?
What was your most successful connection?
Today's experience?

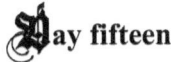ay fifteen

Main theme of the day

The power of assistance

What to use

*Use desire, determination, decisiveness, appetite and
your ability to combine. The power of assistance is the
ability acquired by combining all possibilities in the current time, at the current location and in the current situation.
Take a look around and search one simple situations.
Look at amazing concept, in which is present the power
of assistance.*

Write answers to the following questions
(Describe the situations and your feelings)

*Have you ever experienced disappointment with poorly
provided assistance?
Have you ever experienced perfectly provided assis-
tance?
Have you ever be able to improve something?
If you had something to advise yourself, what would it be
and how would you assist yourself?
Today's experience?*

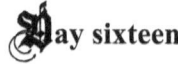ay sixteen

Main theme of the day
The power of seeing

What to use
Use your ability to see (outer and inner). Social situations are often triggered by inconsistency and contradiction. This is due to the variety of physiological vision. Today, however, you will see things as they are.
Choose an object today and observe its geometry. Don't give him an intellectual significance, just look for a while at geometry.
Then choose a life situation and watch how it flows. Just watch and do not interfere.

Write answers to the following questions
(Describe the situations and your feelings)
Have you ever had vision problems (diseases, injuries, or something else)?
What do you prefer to watch?
Have you ever seen something that others could not see?
How would you describe emptiness?
Today's experience?

ay seventeen

Main theme of the day

The power of speech

What to use

*Use your ability to speech (outer and inner). Speaking
(internal and external) is a gift which move this world, or
even more, it revives it. This gift is often negatively
abused, but you use it from this moment in the best possible way.*

*First, choose one social communication that you will
only observing. Second, choose one therapeutic communication that you will only observing. Third, choose one
religionist communication (it is up to you, which philo-
sophical-religious direction you choose) that you will
only observing.*

Write answers to the following questions
(Describe the situations and your feelings)

*Have you ever experienced an insubstantiality communi-
cation?*
*Have you ever met someone with so powerful speech
skills, that you was amazed of it?*
What is your most powerful slogan?
What is the most splendid word you know?
Today's experience?

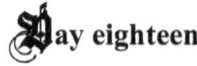

Day eighteen

Main theme of the day

The power of the dive

What to use

*Use your naturalness. You have to dive into the deep of
your mind and that's exactly what you are doing today.
Observe today the constant flow of knowledge contained
in any object or situation (choose only one object or situation).*

Write answers to the following questions
(Describe the situations and your feelings)

*Have you ever been nasty or artfulness?
In which situations are you always natural?
How do you acquire knowledge and skills?
Describe the feeling or feelings when you fall asleep.
Today's experience?*

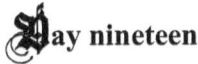

Day nineteen

Main theme of the day
The power of the free will

What to use

Use all your vital functions and ability to relax them.
Free will is most respected possibility you have. You can
compare free will the state of physiological regeneration.
It's the way you can experience real facts.
Today, focus on one of your vital functions and observe it
for a while. Feel all the facts behind it.

Write answers to the following questions
(Describe the situations and your feelings)

Have you ever been in such a physical or mental state
that you needed help from someone else?
How old would you be if you didn't know how old you
are?
When many people say that life is too short, why do a lot
of people say things they don't like and why they like so
many things they don't do?
What was your greatest free will experience?
Today's experience?

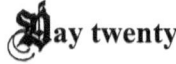 ## ay twenty

Main theme of the day
The power of leadership

What to use

Use your creativity, innovativeness, respectfulness, courage, commitment, confidence, decisiveness, engagement, flexibility, humor, optimism, strategy, vision and other leading skills. Today, something changes, but it retains its essence. You are the very essence of yourself and the change is to strengthen your leadership skills.
Today, find a place where you can observe a landscape lit by the sun.

Write answers to the following questions
(Describe the situations and your feelings)

Have you ever experienced led by an incompetent leader?
What was your best leadership experience?
When many people say that all is said and done, what can you say more?
What does the leadership mean to you?
Today's experience?

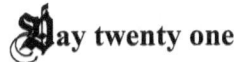

Day twenty one

Main theme of the day

The power of active manifestation

What to use

*Use your intellect, emotions and instinct. Also use your
activity, sharpness, clearness, trust, gratitude and good
influence. Today you understand the manifestation.
Choose any situation you know about being manifested
by you or someone else's request. Observe the whole process of manifesting this situation.*

Write answers to the following questions
(Describe the situations and your feelings)

*Have you ever experienced that you did not manifest
what you asked for?
What is the most exciting manifestation that you have
ever experienced?
Are you doing what you believe in?
What is the one thing you'd most like to manifest for the
world and universe?
Today's experience?*

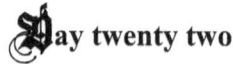 **ay twenty two**

Main theme of the day
The power of closing

What to use

Use skills and abilities you wish for. Today you are in a position to absorb everything in your life experience. Everyone who wants to rule his daily life, must mastering the laws of nature with love. The whole creation, the beginning and the end, you can see everywhere around you. Choose one situation that has already ended. Peacefully observe everything that must happen until it came to its relative end.

Write answers to the following questions
(Describe the situations and your feelings)

Has it ever happened to you that someone "shut the door in front of your nose", which meant the end of the opportunity for success?
If you could offer a newborn child only one advice, what would it be?
What are you most grateful for?
What do you think will happen next?
Today's experience?

After this 22 day system to strengthen renunciation you know, that more giving up of objects from your reality will not help you. Now you see it clearly.

Once you know it and once you have made your personal experience with imagination, inspiration, intuition, visualization and renunciation you are going to use the power of life transformation.

Everything in the universe, in the world and in you, is subject to constant transformation. Transformation is happening continuously and at all levels of nature. The reason behind all of the activity of the nature is to give you practical guidance so that you can transform your life. This is why you should study and have in mind the laws of nature.

You already see the concept of transformation, but have you also understood how the transformation works? How did you change from moment to moment? How did everything around you change from moment to moment? How works transformation from failure situation to big success? How and why do you attract what you have so far? It has escaped your attention because you have trained yourself to act automatically. But now you know it, now you see it, now you live it. You know that you can transform your life either knowingly or unknowingly. It's up to you. No one else will make your transformation, no one else will change you, only you can make the big transformational change in your life. That is why it was used to say "wake up". The only thing what must to awaken in you is your consciousness.

When the consciousness begins to awaken by means of your willpower, you are in the state of all transformational possibilities. To better understand it, you need to know the causes of "sleeping consciousness".

Most people ignore the destructive power of their impressions, their constant need to comment, their constant need to justify and their constant need to judge. Those are the root causes of "sleeping consciousness". That must be over, immediately. Let's have a look for the structure of these four causes.

- *Impressions*

Impressions are the expected result of feelings that you have chosen as true based on your experience. When you woke up in the morning, you maybe took over again and again various alternatives to the situations you have experienced. Maybe you had a negative feelings as fear, worry, anger, dislike, apathy, or good feelings like joy and gratitude. You did not act rationally, you did it so based on your experience with a particular situation. It is because you identified yourself with the impressions you got from that situations (with TV and internet shows, places where you ware, the people you met, food you eat and so on). Ask yourself:

"With what impressions did I enrich myself when I have done it in that way?"

Self-reflection is for sure interesting in this case. What did you come to? What does that say about you? Keep still in mind that what is good for someone else don't need to be good for you. Never ignore the destructive power of impressions. But how to prevent impressions? Let the situations be the situations, let the people be people, let the technology be technology, let the social system be social system, just see everything as it is.

- *Commentary*

Constant need to comment everything is a strange way to show frustration from ignorance. Do you know someone who doesn't need to comment something? Someone who wouldn't express their impressions and opinions? Did you know what that opinions are? They are only another way to express impressions. It have different kind of presentation and manipulation power. Feel them:

"I have an impression" vs. *"I have an opinion"*

Most people need to comment and that is the way of their interpersonal failures. When you woke up in the morning, after the burden of impressions came the various forms of comments on them. You have to give up the need to comment something. To give up in this case means victory and that is a very important fact of your life. Commenting is your ability to show yourself, so use it the best you know in terms of the right time, the right place and the right situation.

- *Justify*

The justification is the answer to your impressions and comments. By justification you deny yourself and I find it very tragic. You are a complete being with all that's belongs to you. You are amazing, you are beautiful, you are powerful and you are unique. If you don't love or put yourself first, who will? You have the right to be as you are. No one can harm you! Stop immediately to have the tendency of justifying yourself whatever you do. Always be you. What can help you in this process? Selecting of seeing situations. That means, you should be aware of what you are looking for. But that does not mean you have to retreat from your daily life. Definitely not. Just be more demanding in what you really want. If you want success, do not look for failure in the form of observations of violence, horror, regret, necessity, excessive consumption and other suggestions and stimulus.

- *Judge*

Judgment is the result of one's own shortcomings or a response to one's own shortcomings. Look around you, how much unnecessary judgment is there. What a waste of life energy. This is all the result of dissatisfaction with the past course of life. It was enough to know before the beginning of every action what everyone wanted (past time) and respect everyone as they are (present time – by respecting you are confirming its uniqueness). Nothing else. It's simple consciousness process.

149

As you could see, each stage multiplies the effects of the previous one. Therefore, one more time, don't ignore the destructive power of impressions, the constant need to comment, the constant need to justify and the constant need to judge. Let everything be as it is.

I often talk about the process of "seeing everything as it is". What are the characteristics of this process "seeing everything as it is"? There is no will and desire, no specification, no imagining, no causality, no duality, no outcome, no time and space limitation, no commitment and no observing.

Example:

If you saw a car before you, you saw it as a car. You did not saw the plane, the train, the apple, your partner or anything else. It was the car. But if you used the car as an object to assess the status of where you were and where you wanted to be, there was a contradiction in your objective and real perception. If you saw a car before you, you saw it as a car. You did not saw the plane, the train, the apple, your partner or anything else. It was the car. But if you used the car as an object to assess the status of where you were and where you wanted to be, there was a contradiction in your objective and real perception. At this time, all of your previous experience – assumptions, requirements, suggestions ("what if, how") -, has been assigned to this car. Also, at this time or point in the time and space, you were out of the process "as it is". It was no longer "as it is", but there was relativity "as it could and should be".

From the previous example, it is also necessary to know that such a process of assigning the importance of a subject attracted to itself also all other experiences, not just yours. In this moment you were the voluntary recipient of all the relative possibilities – someone had to invent the car, someone had to do the design of it, someone had to do the whole process of building it, someone had to transport it from the factory to the dealer, someone had to sell it, someone had to buy it and so on.

You have faced this factors with each assignment of importance. This kind of actions is an extraordinary burden on the mind. Can you imagine what you have been facing in your life so far? What did you voluntarily accepted? What do you consider to be a real life? This is obviously a great awakening for you. What you have so far perceived as life was not a life. It was only a manifestation of volunteered acquired thought patterns of others. Was is bad? For sure not. You already know about it and you've already made a change. This book is not about scaring you, but about to show you other perspective of how to be there, where you want to be.

In order for the transformation to be conscious, it is necessary to realize it. Realization is here more than confirmation, it is the direct handling with the resources available to you. This resources can be and are all the possibilities in and around you. Instead this phrase "realization" you can use description "The realization of our only and true nature". The realization of our only and true nature have its own structure in daily life. You can use following structure to simplify the whole "transformation & realization process".

Realization in your daily life:

1. The reforming of your established habits

You must learn not only to eat and drink to satisfy your physiological needs, but your inner nature as well. Your physical body and your inner world or mental state, are your holly temple for which it is necessary and urgent to take care of it.

Your habits, which you acquire, support and strengthen daily, need to be changed. To do so, you need a powerful and especially functional strategy. One such strategy is "H-DAY". This strategy is successfully used by my clients and friends, who are with its help very successful in transforming their habitual habits. Let me shortly introduce you this strategy.

H – Habits
D – Differentiation
A – Ageless
Y – Youngness

To translate it:

*"**H**abits changing with a focus on its **D**ifferentiation with help of your **A**geless inner **Y**oungness."*

Example:
Changing the habit of drinking coffee

Habit – excessive coffee consumption
Differentiation – selection of activity that is not linked to the need for its repetition
Ageless – timeless situation
Youngness – joyful feeling by new kind of action

To translate it:

Excessive coffee consumption is a habit linked to the compulsive need for its repetition. This repetition must be removed and replaced by non-time-bound activities. This may be, for example, not attending coffee shops for 40 days. This is the way how you make the differentiation. The number 40 is not only a very important symbolic number, but it's exactly the time it takes to get the desired effect in the transformation of your habits, especially when it comes to long term or chronical habits. The "not to attending coffee shops" is the timeless situation in this case. Why? If you do not visit a certain place, of course, you are not bound to repetition anymore. The "joyful feeling of a new kind of action" is, for example, enjoying the time you've acquired by not visiting the old favorite "coffee shop" place.

Joyful feeling enriches you with the enormous energy that is often attributed to children, which do not perceive time, which just do only what make them pleasure.

The reforming of your established habits is your interpersonal process. You have to choose best one for you. I recommend you to make the 40 day process. Never start with long term or chronic habits. It can be counterproductive. Choose a very simple habit at first and transform it. Just replace it with something that makes you happy in 40 day period.

2. Improving the quality of "living a life"

The "Improving the quality of Living a life" is not a one-time activity based on some magic formula. You are constantly improving your life situations whether you are aware of it or not. You should be aware mostly of your thoughts, words and actions. Everything else happens automatically. To improve the quality of "living a life", you can use following ideas:

- Smile
- Be thankful
- Meditate
- Be intuitive
- Exercise in many variations
- Learn something new, something other than usual
- Use autosuggestion possibilities
- Sleep less, relax more, but be in comfortable state
- Eat less, nourish more, but be in comfortable state
- Don't observe your relative lack of something
- Observe joyfulness and success
- Meet people who enrich you
- and so on

3. Creating a big change within your personality

Don't change the others, change yourself. This is the most important to understand. I always say:

"Your change is a change for others."

It's a nonviolent way to create according to your current thought, ideas and needs. There are many acknowledged teachings that try to convince you that you have sharing your personal changes with others. Do not trust in this kind of learning. Your personal change is your personal change, therefore it's also called as a personal and therefore it is not called "shared change". It's your change! If your personal change happened, you'll be amazed and surprised how many questions you suddenly get from people you've never met before. This is a law of similarity.

Why is it not desired to share your personal change or development with others? If you share your intention to change your personality, you are exposing yourself to abuse and re-shaping your real needs. What does it means? It means that you have taken the role of a passive victim and even more, you have denied your nature. Willingly and knowingly, you have accepted the opinions and needs of others as they are your own and you already know from the previous text what such action can cause.

Have also in mind that sharing your needs with others to get feedback, or to get new ideas, or to get help, is something completely different.

To change your personality, you can use following ideas:

- Smile and have a fun
- Change the way you think and the way you are looking at the things or situations around you
- Celebrate the holidays differently
- Know yourself as a connection with the whole universe, because you are the universe
- Love yourself
- Know you are unique
- Give space to perfection and also to imperfection, because everything is so as it is
- Be patient
- Be confident
- Be spontaneous
- Be a good listener, rhetoric and speaker
- Do things in your way
- Change your current dressing style
- Change your body language
- Motivate others

To make a big change is to be attentive to yourself. Big change is really big step without fear and worries. Even a small change is causing huge changes in your personality. To create a big change is to be aware of big change and to be aware of a big changes is to be already changed. My call and slogan for you is:

"Do the best for you to do the best for others."

4. Realizing what you want to achieve in your life

Realizing what you want to achieve in your life means, you must actively, willingly and knowingly search situations most similar to your needs. If you actively, willingly and knowingly search such kind of situations, you have already activated the needed fuel of the creative forces.

To help you better understand it, I have for you one questioning system, which I often use in my practice. It is an extraordinary revitalizing system that can help you get immediate answers to your requirements. All you need for it, is a real interest in yourself.

- If you don't know what you want, ask yourself:

    "What is that, what I do want in this moment?"

    and say to yourself:

    "Everything I do is an expression of my success."

- Identify your passions and ask yourself

    "What does the success mean for me?"

    and say to yourself:

    "Success constantly flows through me."

- Become your own boss and ask yourself:

    "Is this, what I am intend to do, the way to my success?"

    and say to yourself:

    "I am on the right path to my success."

- Travel and ask yourself:

"I know there's something important here. What is it that I'm looking for?"

and say to yourself:

"I am the soul of this place."

- Make a new experience (not life-threatening) and say to yourself:

"I'm always safe."

- Know that the whole world is your playground with unlimited possibilities and say to yourself:

"I love the whole world and the universe."

- Know that you are never alone and say to yourself:

"The whole world and the universe have joined together to help me in all situations."

- Be healthy and say to yourself:

"I am joyful, strong and healthy being."

- Don't compare your life situations to other people's life situations and say to yourself:

"I have unlimited creativity and the ability to create and change everything I want."

- Know that you can be whatever you want and do whatever you want and say to yourself:

"I am a living expression of the absolute."

- Be simple in everything and say to yourself:

  "Simplicity is my naturalness to receive gifts of abun-dance."

- Embrace an attitude of gratitude, because with the power of gratitude you get more from life and say to yourself:

  "Gratitude transforms the moment by shifting me."

- Know the beauty of rejection and say to yourself:

  "I can be whatever I want and I can do whatever I want."

- Know the beauty of blessing and say to yourself:

  "By looking for the blessings in my life, I am in a place of living light in every situation."

- Know the beauty of the greeting and say to yourself:

  "I recognize our true essence in every being."

- Know the beauty of compassion and say to yourself:

  "I am the purest compassion."

- Know the beauty of forgiving and say to yourself:

  "I am in peace with all beings."

- Know the beauty of change and say to yourself:

  "With love and pleasure I enjoy all possibilities."

- Know the beauty of peace and say to yourself:

  "Peace is everywhere I am."

Enjoy the realizing what you want to achieve in your life. It's a beautiful process of your current change. There are also some questions you have to answer seriously:

I.   Why do I want to achieve it?

You have to know why you want to achieve your current requirements. The following questions can help you find the essence of the inner unconscious system, which you can call as "the why perspective system":

- Do you want freedom and joyfulness?
- Do you want to be healthier?
- Do you want to help others?
- Do you want to be more educated?
- Do you want to have extraordinary skills?
- Do you want to be more visible and famous?
- Do you want to experience glory and victory?
- Do you want to prove something to yourself?
- Do you want to be stimulate?
- Do you want to travel more?
- Do you want to replace the lack of something?
- Do you want to have your business empire?
- Do you want to spend more time with your beloved and closest ones?
- Do you want to enjoy life?

Your answers are your treasure and a source of knowledge of what you want to achieve.

II.   When do I want to achieve it?

Second, you have to know when you want to achieve your current requirements. You already know that time is relative and that you have to communicate in the presence. In terms of achieving a specific requirement, it is necessary to realize that manipulation with time is subject to certain laws. In this case of time manipulation, there is only one single law and that law is the "will to have". Yes. The will to have is the particular manipulation key to become successful in time and space.

Example:

If you knew what you wanted, but you said *"I want it anytime"* or *"I do not know when I want it"*, you just confirmed your fear and distrust of achieving it. Why? Because they are expressions linked to the uncertainty of time change. All uncertainty expressions revive countless undesirable effects in life. That's essential to know here. On the other side of this "wanted case example", if you said *"I want it at this particular date"*, you've been exposed to an unexpected stressors. Why? Because you had with this kind of expression absolutely no access to a specific point in the relative future. During the period of pronounced specific requirements, to the point of its relative realization, are present a myriads of options. What a hard way a lot of successful people had to go through, before they achieved their wishing success. Why and what for a hard work. The reason was, because they voluntarily and willingly exposed themselves to all possibilities pointing to a specific date in the time and space until the materialization of the requirement become active.

Therefore, it is necessary that you are free of all uncertainties linked to necessity. Feel the statements or expressions from this example:

"I want it anytime"
(Negative confirmation associated with uncertainty of time change)

"I do not know when I want it"
(Confirmation of the uncertainty at all)

"I want it at this particular date"
(Confirmation associated with expectation of fiction that leads to many unpleasantness and disappointments, until the desired effect occur – the hard way to be successful)

"I want to have it"
(Neutral confirmation ready to be fulfilled)

As you could see, your success is exclusively in your hands. Your success is your exclusiveness! Just choose the right approach, at the right time, on the right place and during the right situation. To make your selections easier, I recommend you to be a very simple and as clear as possible approach to all situations. This is the simplest way that does not contain any resistance. You can use following statement to strengthen your time management capabilities:

"I am constantly in flow with the entire universe"

III. Do I want to achieve it myself or with someone else?

Third, you have to know with whom you want to achieve your current requirements. There are many ways how you can achieve success. One such way is whether you want to achieve your success alone or in cooperation with someone else. Each of these methods requires mainly your full attention. Whether you want to achieve your success alone or with someone else, be attentive. Using attention, you confirm your uniqueness and at the same time activate your protection mechanisms before unwanted mixing of your goals with the goals of others. There is nothing worse than getting into the chaotic and uncontrolled situations of the group. Therefore is in countless texts written the obligate statement "be yourself".

If you have chosen to achieve success alone, the following strategic points can help you:

- *Trust in yourself*

Trust in yourself means trust in everything. If you have trust in everything, there is no possibility or situation that could hurt you.

- *Be yourself*

Become a living manifestation of your thoughts, words and actions. As you already know, your thoughts, words and actions must be in harmony to manifest everything you want. It is impossible to think negatively, to speak negatively and to act negatively and in the same time to be successful. It is impossible to think in one way, to speak and act in another way and at the same time to be successful. In a split way of thinking, speaking and acting, are only undesirable situations achieved.

- *Transform your peace and patience into action*

This is to achieve mastery. If you can transform your peace and patience into action, you have already done your masterpiece of success. A simple way to reconcile peace with patience and transform them into action is to write all the messages you receive during practice of peace and patience. By writing, for example, an idea, a friend's advice, a pleasant situation, or anything else that matters to you, you are confirming your intention to be successful. This writing confirmation is the process of transformation and the act itself. In this way everyone has succeeded.

Example:

Have you ever thought about the process of transformation from failure to success? Being depressed, in anger, in fear and worry or in another emotional mood, one's success began in peace, silence and patience. How that? Very simple. First you have to understand, that being depressed, in anger, in fear and worry or in another emotional mood, is your personal protection you created from your past life experiences. It's a specific and powerful mental state that makes you be able to achieve anything you want, because in it are activated all the necessary mechanisms to make it happen. It's a state of being away from the unpleasant stressor.

The second thing you need to understand is that these mechanisms are an immediate suspension of the current unpleasant situation. You've created it, you've suspend it and you change it for your new strong site and next success. That's why I always say and urge everyone to take all their relative unpleasant situations and turn them into their greatest success.

The third thing you need to understand is that after (in the same time) these mechanisms every time came firstly the silence, second the peace and third the patience (also in the one time). In this triple sequence, there is hidden a secret of success.

The fourth thing you need to understand is that after this triple sequence came impulses or answers for creating or manifesting. How often after relief from unpleasant situation did you get the best ideas, answers, or solutions?

Think about this it for a moment.

- *Do things as different as you can*

Difference has similar effects to those I have described in the previous example. Doing things as different as you can, give you a possibility to be constantly in the process of willing and desired creation or manifestation of success.

- *Give up on trying to look cool*

Many put too much emphasis on looking cool. That's not the way you should take. Looking cool is a fiction and accepting someone else's limitations. You are who you are and therefore you are already cool. You don't need to work on to look cool.

- *Don't create measures to success*

You have surely heard or read that you have to create measurable objectives. I teach my clients and friends exactly the opposite. The reason is very simple and practical. To achieve really quick successes, you should not be limited by measurable goals. The method of measurement is only appropriate if you wish to reach the exact amount, or exact life situation (health, partnership, etc.) to a certain date. I am not writing now about such kind of success. Now I'm dealing with success alone as it is and success alone as it is, is unmeasurable. You are an endless manifestation of the absolute, so why should you set some boundaries and limitations?

Example:

If someone asked for $ 10,000 extra dollars to a certain date, after completing the specific strategy, he or she also "+/-" earned that value. That's a fact. But if the same person said the following *"I want $ 10,000 extra dollars or more, at a certain date."*, then he or she for sure became more than required.

- *Write the way you think about success*

Describe exactly what success means to you. It's an important act to revive your innermost creativity.

- *Know, that the success is you*

To be successful, you have to become a success by yourself. Set that statement right at the beginning of your manifesting process. This will help you see all life situations around you in a different, more creative angle of view.

If you have chosen to achieve success with someone else, the following strategic points can help you:

- *Observe and analyze people you need*
If you have chosen to achieve success with someone else, you must act with the law of similarity. Similarity principles are simple. Choose people who are similar to your mindset. This is how you secure your harmonious teamwork, mutual respect and loyalty.
- *Create a joyful strategic field and stop working hard*
You can create a joyful strategic field only if you determine straight at the beginning that you stop to fight or compete with others and stop working hard. Fighting and competition attracts only further fighting and competition. Hard work attracts only further hard work. Your destination is joyfulness with succeeding and not destruction and hardness!
- *Be yourself, take action and demonstrate a progressive attitude*
You are unique, so stay unique and from this uniqueness you must take action and demonstrate a progressive attitude. In this way, you show your team that you are absolutely competent in what you offer.
- *Use strengths of the team and clarify everyone's strategic role*
Find, transform and use the strongest skills and abilities of your team. Transform them as oneness. Only in that way you can achieve the power of your team.

- *Make a commitment with the team*

In order to work most effectively, you and your team must work as one organism. This requires the establishment of simple commitments:

Everyone in the team is unique;
You are one organism, where each member enriches the whole organism;
Success is the result of joint efforts;

- *Allow constructive communication in the team*

Without mutual communication, successful results cannot be achieved. The communication in your team must take place smoothly and not only on the basis of precise defined business meetings. These are, of course, extremely necessary, but your mutual communication must be flow.

- *Track the goals regularly*

Regular tracking of goals allows you to focus on what you want to achieve, what a progress is done and what else has to be done.

- *Celebrate every single success*

The celebration of each success attracts more success, because there are no small successes. You must be grateful for everything, even if it may seem like an insignificant little thing. This is one piece on the success achieving way how you can get what you really want.

- *Know, that success is the team*

If you have chosen to achieve success with someone else, you must set them all as already succeed. You all as one organism are already a success.

168

Transformation as a concept is big as life itself. Therefore, there are for you endless possibilities you can choose for your personal life transformation.

Once you know it and once you have made your personal experience with imagination, inspiration, intuition, visualization, renunciation and transformation, you are going to use the power of living your life.

Living your life is the knowing of yourself. To know yourself is fundamental. You must use all available options with its full capacity. We all currently live within a very interested mechanism, which is ready for using under our control. Many think there is no final solution. Well they are wrong. The reason they think like this it is that they think, speak and act mechanically and periodically. Only that one who is the slave of mechanicity and periodicity is bound to repeat of his life dramas and can never find the final solution. The final solution means to be not bound at all, it is to be absolutely and conscious free. You need to know how to react towards the different circumstances of your daily life. To know how to react, there are a lot of traditional strategies. I really like to cooperate with my clients and friends on different kind of strategy systems. One of such special strategy systems I would like to introduce you in the following capture.

All interpersonal transformation or development occurs because of the state of energy within you. Learn to use your full energy potential and you can guide your success path. For that reason you need to be especially peaceful.

The willpower and desire are the key to everything you wanted. You, as a manifested human being, have the most varied characteristics. All this characteristic are ruled with willpower and desire. That is why you need to know them, to deal with them, to transform them, to use them, to provide them further, but not play with them. Let the beautiful will of the peace in you be also the beauty in your daily life manifestations. The combinations of your infinite essence are wonderful. All of us are the manifestation of life itself that arise in each heart. The keys are in your hands. At the end of this chapter about willpower and desire, I will give you one more time this question:

"If you believe in achieving your goal, if you can imagine your goal, if you can feel your goal, do you need constantly ask for it?"

Chapter three

"The art to know, transform and manifest."

STRATEGY FOR SUCCESS

𝕬 real life leader sees through people and motivates them by his example. In order to be an example, he must master the art of strategy. In order to master the art of strategy, he must know his own structure of manifestation or reactions in daily life situations. That's the essential.

In this world, it is modern to create and abuse strategies exclusively for competitive environment and competitive fight. Such a way of thinking and acting is destruction itself for everyone. With such thinking and action, you must stop immediately. Before you start to think about something as unrealistic as the competition, try to think over the following explanation for a moment. What is actually a competitive environment and a competitive fight? These are intentionally created terms for destruction. These are the subconscious manipulative means that most of the people have with pleasure accepted. So far, you have been learned from many teachers to differentiate yourself from others in order to become more profitable. But, if someone wanted to create or offer "something better than other competitors" in order to become more profitable, he only created or offered it from the position of his relative current lack of something and from the subconscious need to weaken others for his own profit. This is unacceptable. If you already know that you are unique and that everywhere everything is enough for everyone, the word competition doesn't give a sense. Everything you need to do in the strategic shift process to your success is to create a free and joyful offer without observing "whether it is better or worse than other competitors", or without thoughts "I want to offer it only to good people, not to the bad people". Look at the nature. Nature offers its wonderful gifts to everyone. The nature doesn't think about the competition and whether someone is good or bad, or whether someone deserves it or not. Nature does not fight, nature offers. You are a part of the nature, you are in the nature and the nature is in you. Make it like the nature. Just create a free and joyful offer of the best version of yourself. This is the only real strategy – to offer yourself.

There are several ways of the offering you should know.

- *Offering a little of total ownership for the personal purpose of recognition, or for better personal social status, or to show personal importance*

Offer from calculation is the most abominable way of offering, the most abominable way of strategy.

- *Offering from a whim*

Such a kind of offering brings unexpected losses. This is a kind of strategy is naïve and dangerous for both sides – the offeror and the recipient.

- *Offering of deliberate deception*

Such a kind of offering can bring only all kind of negativity. This kind of strategy strengthens the resistance to itself, to the people, to the whole environment, to the nature and to the whole universe.

- *Offering with suffering*

Such a kind of offering can bring only more suffering. This kind of strategy brings only sadness.

- *Offering of adapting to others*

Such a kind of offering can bring only suffering, slavery and unexpected unpleasant situations. This kind of strategy strengthens slavery of the rules and limitations of others.

- *Offering everything, despite small ownership*

Such a kind of offering brings the abundance. This kind of strategy shows "your own example of sufficiency" and cannot be learned. It's a personality itself.

- *Offering with joy*

Such a kind of offering brings joyfulness. This kind of strategy is supporting "your own example of joyfulness" and reveals the possibilities that have been to this point in time and space overlooked.

- *Unconditional and natural offering*

Such a kind of offering is the only real offering. This kind of offering means "The offering is you". Unconditional and natural offering is not only strategy, it is your way of life and it is to show the best version of yourself.

If you offer the best version of yourself, offer something so unique and amazing, which is for others as a guiding beacon at sea. Therefore, competitive environment and competitive fight does not exist, there can be only groundless fear of lack, envy, anger and hatred. In other words, there is only the ignorance. You should also know, that competitive environment and competitive fight are selfdestructive processes. Everyone who manipulates and use them is exposed to countless threats. That's the fact and that's the law.

As I mentioned at the end of previous chapter, I would like to introduce you one of my strategic systems. This amazing personal mind map strategy system is showing you, what everything you have overlooked, how many possibilities you have, how strong you are and how you can combine them. Name it how you like, because it is your personal identification process.

The aim of this strategy is to reveal your strengths. It is extremely important that you have a conscious approach to your full potential. To get this approach knowingly, you need to first discover it. Once you've discovered it, you can use it as needed.

As with all strategic approaches, we can also by this personal mind map strategy system talk about planning and structuring. Here´s the main structure of that system:

1. The name of strategy

Before you start looking for a name for your strategic system, think about it. I wrote, that you can name it how you like, because it is your personal identification process. When it is your personal identification process, what better title name would you give him if not your own "name and surname"? Your name and surname have big power.

Your name and surname are the result of all the manifestations of all, not only yours, ancestors. There is hidden all the knowledge you need to get where you want to be. This does not mean, that you have to search and work on the entire genealogy of your and other ancestors. Definitely not. Everything you need, you have in this current moment in yourself. It is constantly present in you and ready to help you anytime you want.

You are the result and everything what you are living is the answer to your questions. It's just a game of your social imagination. Especially, keep in mind that your name and surname were manifested at the concrete time and space and therefore look at that exact moment. That moment is miraculous, that moment is a manifestation of your creative energy. That manifested creative energy is your ability to create your own successful life.

Whole life you used your name and surname as your own identification and specification. You used them with absolute certainty, absolute "of course". You used them every time unknowingly and automatically and you did not even know how much power you´ve used.

At the moment of receiving your name and surname, "mental copying" from your ancestors occurred. This was how all the definitions and all the knowledge of your ancestors were copied and confirmed. The assignment of your name and surname was a conscious and wanting act, but it was in the same time also an unknowingly and automatically act. Conscious and wanting, because those who gave you your name and surname had a clear vision of how your name and surname will look like for the rest of your life. Unknowingly and automatically, because all aspects of the universe were not included in the choice of your name and surname. And right here is all your strength and power hidden. Excluding or not thinking about including all aspects of the universe is a allowing to manifest the universe exactly the way you want and need. These are the doors to all your powers. The whole process was hidden between knowing and unknowing. There, in the "space of between", is one option you have to act with. This option is a conscious remembering. You can apply the conscious remembering to all your life situations that are bound to duality. It is a very simple and efficient transformation process.

The following example will show you this interesting process of remembering your natural power.

Example:

The name and surname was considered as "of-courseness". This "of-courseness" need to be connected with the "space between" consciousness and unconsciousness.

Focus on the "of-courseness" of your name and surname. Now, separate the "of-courseness" from your name and surname. The feeling you have reached is your interpersonal description of the "space between". Now, take that feeling, but don't describe it. When you feel comfortable with that feeling, use them for something, you really want. Connect that feeling with the current requirement, which you must see as already done. That's important. As a confirmation you can use following statement:

"It is natural to be ... your statement (peaceful, joyful,
wise, healthy, rich, successful, beautiful, good parent or
partner, teacher, student, etc.)."

Hold this connection of your feeling with your statement and multiply it (that feeling) slowly and easily until you achieve the desired mental effect. After this process, be especially thankful and joyful.

Know, that this is a process and process have to grow. So, use it first for "smaller things" and gradually add to the importance. Know also, it is enough to do this process only one time for every situation.

Think about how often you used your name and surname with "of-courseness". If you used them as "of-courseness" you accepted imaginary boundaries, because the name and surname are used as a standard description of something specific, which is taken as the limited result of many other factors in order to ensure the form of difference and uniqueness (uniqueness in terms of searching your person in the social system rather than uniqueness as unlimited boundlessness).

The power of your name and surname is evident and unquestionable. Use them knowingly, effective and with honor. To strengthen your personal mind map strategy system, incorporate the following "stability of the name and surname" steps into your daily actions:

Know that your whole name is your brand and your personal strategy system

*

Whenever you represent yourself with the whole name, be aware of the amazingness hidden behind it

*

Create a joyful atmosphere with your whole name wherever you are

*

Free yourself of prejudices that someone has a bigger name than yours

*

2. The scheme

The scheme (see the schematic template below) of your personal identification process is very important. Creating such a scheme, clearly shows you all your past, current and relative future "living the life" skills and abilities.

PERSONAL MIND MAP STRATEGY

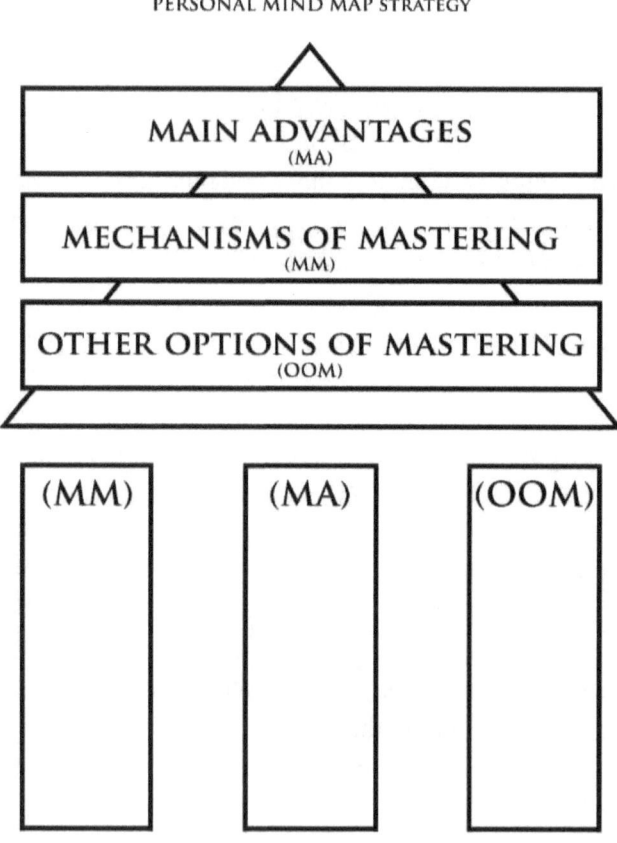

The schematic contains several important details that I am going present to you.

Main geometry of the scheme

One of my favorite activities is to create strategies by using geometric visualizations. For those purposes, I use fundamentally basic geometric shapes that are excellent carriers of all the necessary information values.

As you can see, the basic element of this strategy is a triangle or a pyramid. This traditional element borrows a lot of authors in order to express their strategic thoughts. The reason why a triangle or pyramid is such a popular geometric element is that because it is natural for our mind to use upward visualizations to describe the potential progress or success. Upward is a secret symbol of hope and hope is a hidden meaning of a triangle or pyramid pointing upwards. It's a subconscious program that most people have adopted and therefore you can work very well with it.

You can also see three horizontal pillars on the scheme. These pillars intentionally overlap the triangle or pyramid. It would of course be possible to divide this triangle or pyramid into three spheres, but that would not bring you the desired effect. If you would divide this triangular pattern into three spheres, as used by many other teachers, you would create a clearly-defined boundaries of yourself and you already know that you have no boundaries. Overlapping the triangular pattern with three horizontal pillars gives you the necessary freedom to handle with the whole scheme.

Horizontal pillars also have their individual importance. The meaning lies in their harmonious positioning them, which is no way to distort the basic and pure form of the triangular pattern. They are and also they are not part of the triangular pattern, or in other words, these pillars can be taken as part of an imaginary shift to success, but they do not have to. Exactly placing the pillars, gives you an unlimited opportunity to handle the whole scheme.

Another advantage of horizontally overlapping pillars is the simple and natural ability to name them. It is extremely important that all the primary and main names are clearly legible. This comfort gives you, in particular, their horizontal positioning.

Now we are getting to a very interesting fact. This is the direct manipulation of your life. How? As you can see, the "other" three pillars are placed vertically, containing only shortcuts of the main names. These three pillars are not new or some other main elements of the scheme. They are the same horizontal pillars, but intentionally turned in the vertical direction. If you wish, you can also name them as a sub-elements of the scheme. Why is that so? If you take a fully functional element (in this case your horizontal pillars), that is an element that already has its own name and you turn it into its vertical position (or any other position), while retaining its main part as the main template, you knowingly and willingly manipulate the time and space (with your life, with your success, with your health, etc.). The naming of vertical pillars with shortcuts also has multidimensional relevance and importance.

- First dimension is the "relativity of importance". The human mind has been programmed for reasons of importance for thousands of years (and perhaps many more). Something was "more" important and something little "less" important. In this case, the main themes of horizontal pillars are "more" and the shortcuts on vertical pillars little "less" important. Of course, the importance is the same. You have to know that either something is important or not, no less or more important does not exist and therefore such "importance concepts" must be completely omitted from your thought patterns.

- Second dimension is the "shortcut science". Your main theme must be in harmony with its shortcut form. In this way, you align or harmonize, the overall meaning of the scheme. How? Another of the human mind programs is the searching for logic and harmony. If you set the correct and powerful name of the main theme, it automatically gives you interesting and powerful shortcuts. This is the driving force for all your thoughts. Shortcuts are a mental trigger that gives you access to your schema any time you want and without thinking about the entire title of the main theme. Just have it in your mind.

- Third dimension is a dimension in dimension itself and it is the "multiple meanings of shortcut". Using shortcuts is as old as humanity itself. If you choose the correct and powerful name of the main theme, you gained a shortcut which you can handle as you want and also change the complete importance of the main theme itself. Such a power is behind shortcuts.

- Fourth dimensions is the "vertical grounding". Vertical grounding is another program of the human mind. If you show to your mind that you are taking the horizontal element and then you rotate it to the vertical plane, the mind accept it as an expression of "anchoring" or grounding. In other words, mind takes it as a command to create it or to manifest it. Why? Because you have done something relative unexpected. Your mind has "never before" worked under your command, but of course all of your actions were directed to this conscious point of the big change. You could also say that your unconscious mind did not expect it and the stressor (conscious handling or manipulation with the geometric patterns) have made the needed change. It is a standard creation process due to geometric patterns and that's how your mind routinely works.

Multidimensionality cannot be described in one book because it is constantly under its own changing for your needed personal development. The higher descriptions shows you how amazing creative powers you still have in your hands. The difference is only whether you would like to act routinely or knowingly. Of course, I recommend you to act knowingly.

If I write here about strategy, you have probably noticed that it's more about strategies in the strategy, because each described step in this book can be expanded into its infinite possibilities. Why and how? Because you are infinite and all strategies are only your possibility to manifest parts or patterns of yourself. That's how you lived your life, that's how you created your life, that's who you were.

Main advantages (MA)

The main advantages express your greatest abilities. It can be anything and since this is your personal scheme, there is no system or explanation that tells you exactly what the main advantages are. Of course, for a better understanding and for your comfort by the working with your schema, I will give you some examples from my practice for all three mechanisms which I writing about.

The main advantages are placed as a central pillar. This placement is not accidental but purposeful. As you already know, your mind works with the geometry or images that are presented to it. The central vertical pillar acts as something very important, central, harmonizing and connecting thoughts with acts. It is a combination of feel and thought with the already manifested. The central pillar attracts most of your attention, whether you want it or believe it or not.

For these reasons, it is necessary to write in the center vertical pillar only your greatest abilities. Your abilities deserve your most attention. By writing them on paper or on your computer (it´s on you), you express and confirm their importance. Your mind is from that moment forced to constantly work with them and subject them to all your actions – both, conscious and unconscious. It's a very simple yet powerful tool to modify your old patterns of behavior.

Mechanisms of mastering (MM)

Mechanisms of mastering are your behaviors patterns, which always guaranteed you a safe and satisfying leaving from the unpleasant situation. Even here it can be anything, because everyone is unique and everyone reacts differently to different stressful and unpleasant situations.

Mechanisms of mastering are placed as a left pillar. This placement is also not accidental but purposeful. Your mind, regardless of whether you are right-hander or left-hander, works with a traditionally used geometric placement system. This means that each placement in the space (visible and also relatively invisible) is precisely defined. As like the central vertical pillar attracts most of your attention, the left vertical pillar is automatically mental associated with seriousness. This seriousness is connected with the mechanisms of mastering you have mostly used automatically during unpleasant situations. It is not seriousness in the standard social sense, it is the seriousness or mechanisms of mastering which are multiplied by the fact that these are the gateways from discomfort.

For these reasons, it is necessary to write in the left vertical pillar only your greatest mechanisms of mastering. By writing them on paper or on your computer (it´s on you), as it is in the main advantages, you express and confirm their importance. Your mind is from that moment forced to constantly work with them and subject them to all your actions – both, conscious and unconscious. It is very simple yet powerful tool to soften your old patterns of behavior.

Other options of mastering (OOM)

Other options of mastering are all the additional skills you have gained during your life. Even here it can be anything, because everyone is unique and everyone has learned something different in life, about what one can say that he control it, or what helps him, or what is simply his hobby. These are relaxing situations which you must distinguish from mechanisms of mastering. Mechanisms of mastering are main mechanisms which get you every time (they are 100% guaranteed mechanisms) out of unpleasant situations, while other options of mastering are "only" additional options to the mechanisms of mastering and to the whole schema.

Other options of mastering are placed as a right pillar. This placement is also not accidental but purposeful. You already know that your mind, regardless of whether you are right-hander or left-hander, works with a traditionally used geometric placement system. As like the central vertical pillar attracts most of your attention and the left vertical pillar is automatically mental associated with seriousness, for the right vertical pillar is significant the power of expansion or growth. It is not the expansion and growth in a standard social sense. This is especially the case that everything you have learned so far and what you already master, is (whether you are aware of it or not) helping you achieve your desired success.

For these reasons, it is necessary to write in the right vertical pillar only your other options of mastering. By writing them on paper or on your computer (it´s on you), as it is in the main advantages and mechanisms of mastering, you express and confirm their importance. Your mind is from that moment forced to constantly work with them and subject them to all your actions – both, conscious and unconscious. It is very simple yet powerful tool to change your old patterns of behavior and to enrich your current potential.

I could write about these three pillars one or more separate books, but without concrete examples, they would be only theoretical and philosophical assumptions. To theoretize is not my intention and therefore I have chosen a shorter description of the three vertical pillars. Therefore I will give you promised examples from my practice.

Examples for MA / MM / OOM
Example one: Michelle (employment – retail salesperson)

PERSONAL MIND MAP STRATEGY

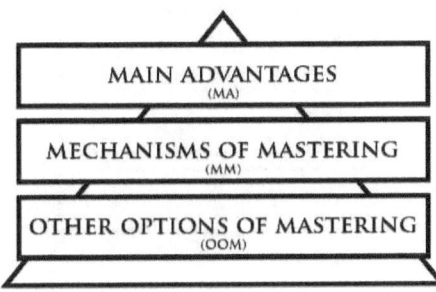

(MM)	(MA)	(OOM)
Archery	Fun	Cooking
Traveling	Creativity	Teachable
Book reading	Detail-oriented	Passionate
Listening to music	Intuition	Sincere
Singing	Communication	Health care
Eating chocolate	Trading	Technical skills
Cycling		Design
Origami folding		
Yoga practices		
Meditation		

Example two: Vladislav (employment – police officer)

PERSONAL MIND MAP STRATEGY

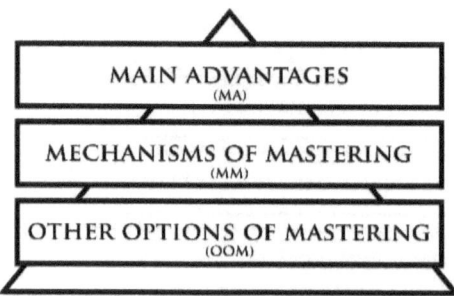

(MM)	(MA)	(OOM)
Shooting	Respect	Technical skills
Traveling	Communication	Teamwork
Fishing	Strong work ethic	Giving presents to others
Eating	Critical thinking	Listening to others
Fun	Logical thinking	Accountable
Watching movies	Resourceful	Dynamic
Home Improvement	Diplomatic	Adaptable
Christmas Eve	Sport	
Sleeping		

Example three: Peter (employment – life coach)

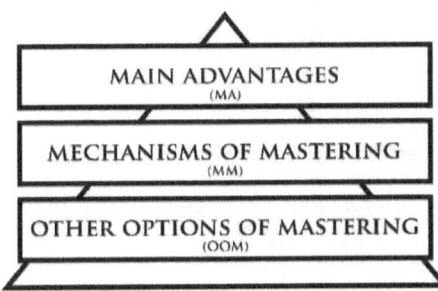

(MM)	(MA)	(OOM)
Traveling	Patience	Listening to others
Realxing 1. on the sun 2. on the beach 3. in the nature	Communication	Philosophy
	Manipulation	Social Sciences
Pipe smoking	Lucky	Buying and selling
Learning new skills	Efficiency	Drawing
Muscle car driving	Teachable	Cleaning
TV watching	Sociable	
Dancing	Positive	
	Sport	

3. Your personal program

A personal program is something that always helped you. It's something so huge and at the same time so gentle that you haven't notice it until today, therefore it can be any of your verbal or internal statements.

Here are examples from my already mentioned clients:

Example one: Michelle (employment – retail salesperson)
On my question, "What was behind all the successes that you have achieved?" came the spontaneous answer:

> **"Good feelings has always brought me the perfect effect."**

Example two: Vladislav (employment – police officer)
On my question, "What was behind all the successes that you have achieved?" came the spontaneous answer:

> **"After the hardness always came the longing effect."**

Example three: Peter (employment – life coach)
On my question, "What was behind all the successes that you have achieved?" came the spontaneous answer:

> **"Perseverance has always given me freedom."**

Would you like to hear, what was my biggest personal program, which constantly accompanied me with my daily life? It's simplicity in itself, but formulated into this statement:

> **"I just achieved it all and that's it."**

4. Goal settings

Goal settings is the process of entering and manifesting your desires into the current time and space. I've already written something about goal settings, but here and now I'm providing you with information for your interpersonal needs.

- Be general

Do you want a million dollars? Why so little? Why limit yourself when you are unlimited? Establish a requirement for financial freedom and let the success be yourself. Become a millionaire with a statement like this: *"I'm a millionaire"*. Repeat it as often as you can, because *"I am a millionaire"* must become you and you must become him. That's the only way. Everything else must go aside. Either you want it or not. Like this, act with everything you want, but if you have really the need to work with the word "million dollars", then better say *"million dollars or more"*.

- Don't set the importance to the goal

You are important enough, so why set the importance to something imaginary? Never identify with the importance, identify only with yourself. If you have already expressed your request by setting a specific goal by no concreteness, then the next logical step should be importance. This is what many teachers teach. But that's not true at all. The relative next step is to be aware of the peace and silence that follows itself (automatically) after setting the concrete goal. In other words, think about the moment that follows

192

the word, sentence of visual picture. Is it peace or silence or not? And straight this peace and silence must be a conscious act of your understanding. This conscious understanding of peace and silence is the confirmation of all work that was done to this moment.

- *Act in accordance with your personal program.*

If you know your personal program, use it for everything you think, use it for everything you talk about and use it for everything you do. This is a way to be connected with yourself and this is the way to be connected with the process of manifestation.

- *Let the result appear.*

Time and space doesn't exist, so you must work with the presence. There is a big psychological difference between that, if you say that you want something reach to a specific date and between that if you want it in the relative general time and space. I give you now an example and you should feel the difference.

Example of "relativity of the reaching"

"I want a million dollars to the date of 01.01.year."

Or is effective to say

"I want a million dollars to the end of this month."

Or is effective to say

"I have a million dollars in this month."

Or is effective to say

"I am a millionaire."

I introduce you next geometric tool gift for your better understanding of this goal setting process.

Goal Setting Process

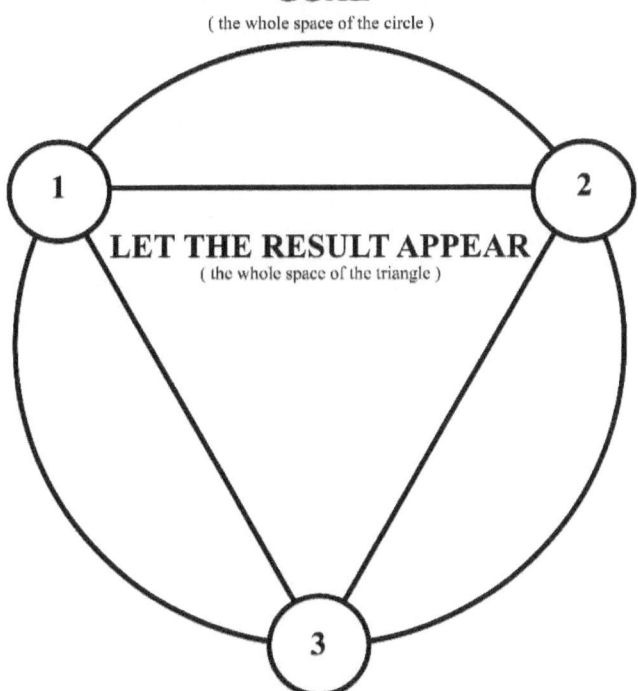

GOAL
(the whole space of the circle)

LET THE RESULT APPEAR
(the whole space of the triangle)

1

2

3

1. Be general
2. Don't set the importance to the goal
3. Act in accordance with your personal program

5. Awareness of "bad habits"

Awareness of "bad habits" guarantees you to handle at the current time everything that has happened and what can happen. This is a simple refinement procedure. Initially, it's a good idea to learn gradual refinement to get a powerful view of transforming "bad habits". Many have tried to transform their "bad habits" immediately, but this has mostly lead to disappointment. That is why I am giving you a clear example of how to learn this important transformational process.

Examples of refinement

These examples are an authentic indicators of how my clients and friends have achieved what they most desired. During reading these examples, be aware of the amazing process of emotional refinement. It's really phenomenal and easing process.

Transformation of success

"Bad habit"
"I still do not succeed in anything."

The first level of gradual refinement
"So far, I have not succeeded."

The second level of gradual refinement
"Everything I did showed me how to succeed."

The third level of gradual refinement
"Everything I do is making me successful."

Transformation of "bad habit"
"I'm absolutely successful, because I'm the success it-self."

Transformation of health

"Bad habit"
"I'm still sick."

The first level of gradual refinement
"I have often been sick so far."

The second level of gradual refinement
"My way of life has taught me how to be healthy."

The third level of gradual refinement
"Thanks to my lifestyle I am in great shape and healthy."

Transformation of "bad habit"
"I'm absolutely healthy, because I'm the health itself."

Transformation of mental disorientation

"Bad habit"
"I'm still in the position of the victim. I do not like my life."

The first level of gradual refinement
"Often I used to be a victim, but I always got out of it."

The second level of gradual refinement
"I have a valuable life experiences, thanks which can I every time be helpful to myself and others."

The third level of gradual refinement
"Thanks to my valuable life experiences I have everything I want."

Transformation of "bad habit"
"I'm absolutely aware of my life, because I'm the life itself."

Transformation of "bad communication"

"Bad habit"
"I am still jumping the others into speech."

The first level of gradual refinement
"Often I interrupted others while they were talking."

The second level of gradual refinement
"I have a wonderful gift of eloquence, which I use at the right time, on the right place and with the right people."

The third level of gradual refinement
"Thanks to my eloquence I'm a searchable and popular speaker."

Transformation of "bad habit"
"I'm absolutely aware of my speech, because I'm the communication itself."

Transformation of impatience

"Bad habit"
"I am impatient in every situation."

The first level of gradual refinement
"In many situations, I was impatient."

The second level of gradual refinement
"I have great ideas with which I can make happy and successful myself and the others."

The third level of gradual refinement
"Thanks to my great ideas, I am happy and successful."

Transformation of "bad habit"
"I'm absolutely aware of timelessness, because I'm the eternity itself."

Transformation of the fear of what the others think

"Bad habit"

"I'm afraid of what the others think of me"

The first level of gradual refinement

"Often I was afraid of what the others thought about me."

The second level of gradual refinement

"I am amazing personality with extraordinary skills that make me very interesting and exceptional for others."

The third level of gradual refinement

"Thanks to my personality I'm a popular teacher."

Transformation of "bad habit"

"I'm absolutely aware of my amazingness and uniqueness, because I'm the unique itself."

As an expressed confirmation you can use at the end of every transformational process following statement:

Expressed confirmation

"I love the whole world and the whole universe,
I love myself and all beings,
I love everything manifested and also unmanifested,
I love that I am,
I love that we are."

Don't forget, that the absolute confirmation is the conscious peace and silence after the end of each process. Just enjoy the peace and silence.
In the moment of mastering this transformation of your "bad habits" process, create your own way of refining.

6. Weekly self-questioning

Weekly self-questioning is very helpful tool especially if you were a beginner in the creating your own personal mind map strategy system. This is a confrontational system of well-defined questions from the four main areas of your life. Who do you confront? Your mind. By this periodical questioning system, is your mind forced to open also such of doors that have been out of your horizons so far. As you already know, time and space do not exist and therefore there is also no periodicity. To understand it better, you have to realize that until you have reached everything you desired, you ere manifested only in the potential state of absolute expression, as the manifestation of past decisions. You are still manifestation of the absolute, but you have been in limited mode. Therefore we can easily say, that the time exists only for those manifestations that are in their potential state and space is between them.

With this weekly self-questioning system you are able to get closer to your real inner essence. It also guarantees you to get out of the place where you are, to where you want to be. Weekly self-questioning has its own form and rules of finding the right questions, to get the best result. Many authors used psychologically constructed questions, or have combined many systems together. This is not the case for the system that I am introduce you and which is also successfully used by my clients and friends. This system is built on the four most important areas of your life: **1.** *the level of all possibilities in potential state,* **2.** *the level of* *knowledge in potential state,* **3.** *the level of forming success in potential state* and **4.** *the level of all actions in potential state.*

First self-questioning area
(The level of all possibilities in potential state)

Main question areas
- Look back, what you wanted and desired for?
- Look back, what you were thinking about, what you were talking about and what have you done?
- Look back, how did you feel?

Possible questions
- What does gold mean to you?
- What does birth and unborn mean to you?
- What does water mean to you?
- What does self-existence mean to you?
- What does universe mean to you?
- What does your body and mind mean to you?
- What does life mean to you?
- What does nutrition mean to you?
- What does moving and nonmoving mean to you?
- What you wanted and desired in the last week?
- Of what you have thinking about, what you have talking about and what have you done in the last week?
- What was the strongest feelings you had last week?
- How would you describe this 12 questions?

Second self-questioning area

(The level of knowledge in potential state)

Main question areas

- Look back, what everything you already know?
- Look back, how often did you used questions and get the answers?
- Look back, did you try to think about the reasons for human existence?
- Look back, did you try to get to know yourself?

Possible questions

- What does good and evil mean to you?
- What does Adam and Eve mean to you?
- What does to see, to know and to experience mean to you?
- What does the beginning and end mean to you?
- What does the education mean to you?
- What does the intuition mean to you?
- What does the concentration mean to you?
- How often have you used the power of concentration and meditation last week?
- Have you been confronted with joyfulness and suffering, health and sickness, youthfulness and aging, birth and death, generosity and greed, humility and pride, love and hatred, courage and fear and with honesty and delusion last week?
- Did you used a different perspective of your daily life situation last week?

- What kind of book/-s did you read last week?
- To what extent you needed some kind of art technique last week in order to know something?
- What have you learned last week and what knowledge you acquired?
- What did you make the most enjoyable last week?
- If you knew anything was false or untruth, did you renounce to communicate about it last week, to save others before a potential disappointment?
- Have you been a good example to others last week?
- To what extent you took advantage of intuition last week?
- Does the peace and silence allowed you to make an intuitive action last week?
- What was the most important thing in the last week for you?
- What unexpected happened to you last week?
- Who was the most important person for you last week?
- When did you feel most relaxed last week?
- How would you describe yourself after all experiences from the last week?
- How would you describe others after all experiences from the last week?
- How would you describe the whole life after all experiences from the last week?
- If you have only one minute left to know something or someone, what would you do?
- How would you describe this 26 questions?

Third self-questioning area
(The level of forming success in potential state)

Main question areas
- Look back, how did you use your senses?
- Look back, how conscious did you use the place and space where you live?
- Look back, what did you have manifested to this day?

Possible questions
- What does all-round success mean to you?
- What does intent mean to you?
- What does mortality mean to you?
- What does inner integrity mean to you?
- What does it mean for you to take responsibility for your own life?
- What does this statement "Nothing is impossible, unless you think it is" mean to you?
- Did you go to nature last week?
- Which of your senses did you used most last week?
- What did you most observed last week and whom do you most often met last week?
- How many ideas did you have to create something new last week?
- Have you attributed to something or to somebody a value last week?
- How many times did you appreciated the place where you live last week?

- How many times did you appreciated the whole world and universe last week?
- Were you satisfied with choosing your profession last week?
- Have you produced something beautiful last week?
- Did you identify yourself (thoughts, words, actions) with something or with someone last week?
- How often you paid attention of yourself last week?
- How often have you used creativity last week?
- How often have you used humor last week?
- What exertion to change (by your own will) you done last week?
- What best solution you done last week?
- What best conception you done last week?
- What best aspiration you done last week?
- Who was the most successful person that you met last week?
- Did you work with attention, love and interest last week?
- Have you been patient last week?
- Did you neutralized the tendency toward mechanical habit last week?
- Did you tried to choose a simple skill that you have never mastered and determined to succeed in it last week?
- What is one thing you're going to do differently after reading this 28 questions?
- How would you describe this 29 questions?

Fourth self-questioning area

(The level of all actions in potential state)

Main question areas
- Look back, have you been abstained in your mental and physical actions?
- Look back, were your actions a reflection of your past thoughts, or your thoughts were reflections of your actions?
- Look back, were your actions subjected of cyclic repetition, or other kind of repetition?

Possible questions
- What does abstaining mean to you?
- What does sexuality mean to you?
- What does this statement "Everything is as it is" mean to you?
- What does to create good conditions for your own personal development and for the all-round goodness of others mean to you?
- What does the necessity mean to you?
- What does your behavior mean to you?
- What does recurrence and return mean to you?
- What does observation mean to you?
- What does family and friends mean to you?
- What does physical activity mean to you?
- What does overcoming mean to you?
- What does escape mean to you?

- What would you say about yourself based on whom you meet until this day?
- What would you say about yourself based on what you own (both materially and mentally) right now?
- How would you describe the difference between "social you", the "private you" and the "inner you"?
- Are you living the life you want?
- What was the most frequent mental and physical actions you did last week?
- What kind of consequences of your actions you experienced last week?
- What kind of opportunities did you look for last week?
- What did you do last week to be successful?
- Did you serve your community last week?
- Did you overcome some opposition last week?
- What motivated and inspired you most last week?
- Would you describe last week as "wisely used"?
- Do you have anything granted last week?
- Did you push the boundaries of your comfort zone last week?
- What was your favorite way to spend the days in the last week?
- Was for you important to love or to be loved last week?
- What did surprised you the most about your daily life last week?
- What would you do today if there is no more tomorrow?
- How would you describe this 30 questions?

7. Daily record of important information values

Daily record of important information values is a real miraculous tool on your successful journey. It is a great form of self-reflection and reflection of the whole day. The most important points that you should record are:

- *Dreams*

Dreams are an integral part of the life process and at the same time they are with the "dejavu" the least understood communication system. Dreams are beyond the power of your will and that's the reason, why it is in this days so abnormally huge market about it. It has become business and nothing else.

You have to know about the dreams especially that they are a real solutions to everything you've experienced in the past. Just direct them (I write about their direction in the following point eight – the precognition). It's the same process as driving a car. The car can become a great helper, but it can also become a killer.

Once the daily life actions are complete, the only thing left are the relative values of duality. In accordance with the law of relative repeating (the whole life process you live), it is certain that the relative values of duality return. They are in re-embodied state, unless you allow it them or unless you don't direct them.

Dreams are the experience of another fact that is your integral part you did not know and experienced so far. The beginner's language of dreams is absolutely comparable to the language of analogy. Just be patient and in any case do not let your dreams interpret from someone else. It's your interpersonal responsibility and necessity to understand them. Do not put yourself in the position of a muddled slave by somebody else's precondition information values. If you let the dreams language be your interpersonal communication, they will become in that moment an identical communication with your reality.

That's the reasons, why you need to pay attention of your dreams and put their values into your daily record.

- *DejaVu*

DejaVu is a recognition system to establish your harmonious state. It is the perfect answer to your perfectly asked question at the right time, on the right place and with the right people. Do you think you did not ask a question? Think about it for a moment. Are not all your needs and requirements an unspoken but manifested questions? The response system or "dejavu" act in this case as follow. If you think about some questions, needs, or requirements without acting in their favor, no answer or "dejavu" will ever come. But if your actions (daily life living) are focused in the direction of your questions, needs, or requirements, the perfect answer or "dejavu" is already on the way to you. What everything you did to make this moment happened?

In the moment of "dejavu", you have the advantage to acting differently to change your reality. That's amazing fact!

The more you consciously experience these moments, the more you consciously understand all the manifestations of your daily life. That's the reasons, why you need to put your "dejavu" values into your daily record.

- *All the most significant situations of the day*

This includes all your experiences that you considered these were significant for you. In addition to these, there belongs also a mathematical and often ezoterized theme of repeating numbers. All mathematical and other repetitive indicators are only the supportive programs of your mind, which show you that you have acted in accordance or harmony with your nature. Just be more attentive. You must also know that these supported mechanisms will only be activated until you realize that you can do everything without them. This is basically a response to your concerns and need to have confirmations from around for everything you do. Stop with that kind of behavior patterns and believe in your amazingness.

- *Personal comments*

Personal comments serve to generalize all the details you wrote. It's a disposable result of the day. Do you need to generalize and close the day from a different perspective? Great! You can write it in one word, which I often recommend to my clients and friends, but of course you can describe it how you need, or also you don´t need to describe it. It's absolutely up to you, it´s your interpersonal system. All you must to have in your mind is that everything you did, you did the best you knew.

8. Predestinations and precognitions

At first, make a list of 108 things that make you smile, because before you really start to predestinate and predict, you have to be able to enjoy being here.

The second, describe yourself with 22 words, because after the feeling of joyful smiling, you have to be in communicative connection with your inner self.

The third, write 33 questions about yourself. All the 33 answers must be composed positive, powerful and motivating to you. This is the way you are able to give and receive answers at the right time, on the right place and with the right people.

Predestination

Predestination is a way of manifesting desirable situations. You can predestine in different ways. It's again something that's just yours. However, the basic structure is as follows.

Example of predestining a safe and prosperous day

Before you step into your day, determine how that day should look like.

"Let this day be safe and prosperous for me in all directions. Let all the situations I experience in this day, be absolute blessing for me. Let this day be refreshing for me.

That's what I want,
That's what I desire,
That's what I wish,
and so it is."

Example of predestining a successful business meetings
Before you start the business or other meeting, determine how that should look like.

"Let this meeting be a joyous and successful start for my
prosperity. I only want good and positive news.
That's what I want,
That's what I desire,
That's what I wish,
and so it is."

This kind of predestining you can use also before you start a business or any other call. If you have already received a call, you can easily say "Please wait for a moment" and tell yourself the mentioned (or any other) statement. After this statement peacefully continue the conversation.
Don't forget, there is always the possibility of transforming the situation, even if it seems difficult.

Example of predestining a "missed" opportunity
If you know that time and space doesn't exist, there are also no missed opportunities. There may have been situations that seemed to be a missed opportunities, but that's just a one-way description of your dissatisfaction of the result and leaving the situation in the hands of someone else. If you don't predestinate, you automatically get into the state of victim and the slave. This is often incorrectly called random action. Such actions and behavior patterns

must be immediately transformed into the predestination process.

After situations that did not brought you the desired success, determine how they should look like. Remember and imagine (only very short) the undesirable situation. Now, change the entire unwanted process to the process as you wanted it should be and say to yourself:

"This amazing experience brings me absolute joyfulness and satisfaction and everything I imagined, or something even better.
That's what I want,
That's what I desire,
That's what I wish,
and so it is."

Example of travel predestining
Before you sit in your car or other transport possibilities, determine how that travel should look like.

"I want a safe and reliable travel with my safe and reliable car. Let this travel be refreshing for me, without any traffic or any other limitations. Let this travel be a blessing for me and let me be in the final destination absolute joyfully and healthy.
That's what I want,
That's what I desire,
That's what I wish,
and so it is."

Predestination is your amazing ability to transform whatever you want. If you begin to predestinate, your life becomes as rich at the moment as you could not even imagine. Just learn the right communication with yourself. This is your only task. Learn to understand yourself. Nothing more, nothing less. You do not have to be forced into the endless studies of philosophical, psychological, scientific, esoteric or other disciplines. Do it as simply as you can. I constantly repeat my clients and friends:

"Beauty is in simplicity."

Predestination and simplicity go hand in hand with your interpersonal communication skills. Just notice what kind of communication makes you more joyful, healthy, harmonious, successful and brings you everything you want. It's a system that gives you an immediate response. That is how it works. Immediately. You do not have to wait for "miracle", only look at the results or manifestations of your past communication skills. That is all.
You can also use the following statement to enhance your capabilities:

"I know that I know.
I know that I can have what I want, to change what I want, to be what I want and to give as much as I want. It's me, it's us, it´s wonderful."

Precognition

Precognition is another interesting possibility you have still in you. It's such a wonderful process that after you get to know him, you will say "Why didn't I use it until now?" This is probably because the subject of the precognition was considered as something extraordinary, or charlatanism, or even sacred and occult. But these are only misleading and deliberate disinformation to hold you back from your all natural possibilities. Precognition is so simple and obvious that there is no need further to write about it as about something that is only for the "chosen ones".

Here is my description of this interesting possibility. Precognition can be divided into *daytime precognition* and *night precognition*. Since night precognition is relatively simpler for beginners, I will begin with this description as the first one.

- *Night precognition*

I have already wrote something about the importance of your dreams. Another way of handling with your dreams is a night precognition. Following is the training, which I do with my clients and friends.

Example training of the night precognition

These are three basic steps to proceed in order to achieve the best results:

NP1 – *Relaxing of mind and body*

Before you fall asleep, relax your mind and body in your way. It is important to have your personal comfort without disturbing elements.

NP2 – Formulation the question you want to know the answer to

The question must be clear and distinct, with the necessity of emotional feeling, because it is an input algorithm. This means that it must be the question you really need to answer. It never should be a questions just for fun or just to try something "new", or to harm someone – not negative at all! If you ask a question with a lack of emotional charge or with negativity, you will receive an adequate (for your current intellect incomprehensible) answer.

The good news is that answers come to every question. That's great news, because it's also an instant indicator of what you asked for. It's basically also an explanation of your life and the statement that you are the result of your past thoughts, words and actions.

NP3 – Confirmation

Confirmation is a statement of how the answer should appear. It is the determination of the output algorithm.

Following is the whole process of questioning and confirming that helped my clients and friends in their beginning practice until they found their own input and output algorithms:

"I want to receive the answer to my question as soon as I fall asleep. I want that the answer is to me clear, distinct and unambiguous in order to understand it. When I wake up, let it is in any way, I want to remember and understand the answer. That's what I want."

Precognition is no clairvoyance or "witchery". It is not a disruption of the nature laws and it absolutely does not mean to "play a god´s role". Think about it for a moment. Once you know that time and space doesn´t exist, about what "miraculous abilities" should we talking about? Precognition is just a downloading the currently required relevant information value from the field of all your options that are in the potential state of manifestation. Nothing more and nothing less.

How come that answers can come through dreams? The answer is simple. Your consciousness does not distinguish between the state of physiological sleeping and the state of physiological awakening. The difference is only that in the state of physiological sleeping, your defensive mechanisms (your old limiting habits - the boundaries of your ego) are automatically "turned off". That's why you are there (in the state of physiological sleeping) in a state where you are able not only to receive all answers for your desired questions, but also to create and manifest directly everything you want. And where all answers come from? Well, from your own and real I!

Night precognition is for many people the first experience that they are capable of things they thought were only for some "chosen ones". You are not limited! You are unique and borderless being, so do not even set boundaries.

Of course, be aware of your precognition requirements, because the answers come to all your every asked questions.

You should also know, that there is no pattern, which questions should be answered and which don´t. There is only one law:

"Who is ready to ask, is also ready to receive adequate answer."

- *Daytime precognition*

Precognition during the day is a very specific system of gathering specific information values. It's real essence extracting from a particular situation or moment. Following is the training, which I do with my clients and friends.

Example training of the day precognition

These are three basic steps to proceed in order to achieve the best results:

DP1 – Focusing and relaxing

Focus on the specific situation or moment in which you want to see (receive) the answer. Your focus must be hand in hand with peace, quiet and relax.

DP2 – Formulation the question you want to know the answer to

The question must be (as by the night precognition) clear and distinct, with the necessity of emotional feeling, because it is an input algorithm. In the case of daytime precognition, you have to be especially precise in your questions, because your ego and all past habits are in activity. Focusing and relaxing are the activities No.1 that help you avoid unwanted past activities or old "bad habits".

DP3 – *Confirmation*

Confirmation in the daytime precognition is a statement of how the answer should appear, but it must be done more carefully as by night precognition. It is also the determination of the output algorithm and therefore, while the ego and old habits are still in activity, you have to choose specific words to avoid unwanted manifestations.

Following is the one basic process of questioning and confirming that helped my clients and friends in their daytime precognition practice until they found their own input and output algorithms:

"I want this situation to be a clear, distinct and unambiguous response to my question. Let the answer be so clear that everything else ceases to exist. In the moment I received the answer, I want to manage it best way as I know for my all-round enrichment and satisfaction. That's what I want."

Daytime precognition is science itself and therefore you must practice with a proper attention. I also do not advise you to praise yourself before others with your results. It is your interpersonal possibility and ability to see all needed answers before the specific and concrete situations in the relativeness of time and space can appear. It's a very powerful weapon of (no only) businessmen that you have right now in your hands. At the same time I encourage and urge you to the laws of ethics and decency. Act constantly with the best intentions for yourself and to all beings. This is the only way to remain joyful and satisfied in every practice with this amazing predestination and precognition systems.

I often write that you have to find your own way of communicating with yourself so you can get what you ask for. What do I mean by this? Is there a way to get it? Is there a system to get it? The way and the system are all your behavioral patterns. Only you are the answer to all wanted questions. I give you an example.

Example

Detection strategy of the effectiveness of behavioral patterns:

- Which words have I used most often and what did I get from them?
- Which kind of reactions on situations I used most often and what did I get from them?

In order to learn to communicate with yourself and to get what you want, you need to be in the joyful or more playful patience. I have often heard from different people that the beginnings are difficult. This kind of thinking was just programming of the fictive beliefs and prejudices. Replace the difficulty for joy and playfulness. Everything is as simple as you set it up. That's what I still recommend you – simplicity, joyfulness and playfulness.

9. The main strategy

The main strategy is the capability combining the acquired information values. In the main strategy, you change your reality.

It is the ability to consciously combine, which gives you the privilege of having your whole life in your hands. But what is actually being combined? Energy, matter and consciousness. That's what you combine. Everything else are just the details of these three components. If you have gathered all information values from your personal mind map strategy system (as mentioned above – Name of strategy, The Scheme, Your personal program, Goal settings, Awareness of "bad habits", Weekly self-questioning, Daily record of important information values, Predestinations and precognitions), you can start to observe all these information values, which is actually the process of conscious combining. Of course, you can also enrich this strategic system with a number of other components, such as personal statements (often referred to as affirmations), adopted functional strategic systems (from someone else, but adjusted to your own needs) and so on.

The creative process is not a singular vision produced by yourself, so there is no reason that different types of information values must be separated or isolated. Final product is created with your ability to combining and it is something people still did without even thinking about it.

For a better understanding of the combining process, I give you the following example.

Example: Michelle (employment – retail salesperson)

Michelle came to me with the following request.

Request: How to increase sales?

Name of strategy: Michelle

The scheme:

PERSONAL MIND MAP STRATEGY

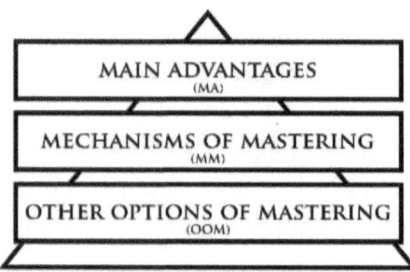

(MM)	(MA)	(OOM)
Archery	Fun	Cooking
Traveling	Creativity	Teachable
Book reading	Detail-oriented	Passionate
Listening to music	Intuition	Sincere
Singing	Communication	Health care
Eating chocolate	Trading	Technical skills
Cycling		Design
Origami folding		
Yoga practices		
Meditation		

Personal program: Communication has always brought me better ways to succeed.

"Bad habits and beliefs" (*I deliberately select only the most important "bad habits and beliefs"*)**:**

- *Habit* – "Every time I am holding myself back from outer world in separation of my room after failure."
- *Belief that held back from succeed* – "There are bigger and stronger companies than my company, so how could I succeed among them?"

The main transformational process

First step was transformation of habits and beliefs

Old habit
"Every time I am holding myself back from outer world in separation of my room after failure."

New habit
"I'm more open to communicating with the outer world because I know everything is heading to my desired success."

Old belief
"There are bigger and stronger companies than my company, so how could I succeed among them?"

New belief
"I and my company are one and therefore I am successful in every area in which I do business. The unity is my strength."

The second step was to find a common element of success with all interpersonal information values

- Combination of *personal program* with *MA, MM* and *OOM*

As you can see, the main theme of *personal program* was the communication. But communication is placed at the personal mind map strategy in the central pillar and on the fifth place. What to do with that? First, it is necessary to establish a connection between the **strongest advantage** and the *personal program*. The result was joyful communication. That was of course not everything. It was necessary to acquire the ability/-s which constantly support the joyful communication. This is in the central pillar seen in the main advantages between fun and communication – creativity, detail-oriented and intuition, plus the last placed trading advantage. Because I very often use the opposite course of the strategic process, the final result was as follow:

"Joyful communication supported with intuitive detail-oriented creativity which lead to successful trading."

At the moment of this result, the other two pillars (MM and OOM) become a completely different meaning than at the beginning of creating this personal mind map system. At this moment, all supportive activities from MM and OOM pillars become the engine for getting the desired result, which was the sales increasing. It was interesting to see what connections arose from the resulting statement.

Third step was acknowledgment in the daily life. This means that it was necessary to act in the sense of the received information values (answers).

Big turnover and desired increase of sales occurred after Michelle's exploration tour ("travel" in the MM pillar) of India, where she learned ("teachable" in the OOM pillar) some new skills. She has incorporated these skills into her business strategy. Some of these skills were the colorfulness ("design" in the OOM pillar) of cooking ("cooking" in the OOM pillar), meditation, yogic skills and singing (all in the MM pillar) and some others.

All this led to a better ability to be at the right time, at the right place and with the right business partners, which automatically led to increased sales.

As you can see, this system of your personal mind map strategy is very simple and determines you to be successful. You have to be to yourself and others honest and true and be attentive to all opportunities which are daily offered to you. You have been able to verify by direct strategy experience that it was difficult to comprehend how success works without comprehending your old behavioral patterns. To know how to know was very difficult. But it doesn't matter anymore. You already have a strategic system in your hands. You already have the keys from the door leading to happiness in your hands.

You know, in the main strategy, you immediately change your reality.

10. Achieved strategic success

You already achieved a success? Great! Write all the details of how you achieved it. This will help you in every life situation. Linking or connection all of your life situations is obvious and when you already have a system that clearly shows you how have you achieved something desired, it also shows you how you can anytime achieve anything else.

As I mentioned on the beginning of this chapter, a real life leader sees through people and motivates them by his example. In order to be an example, he must master the art of strategy. In order to master the art of strategy, he must know his own structure of manifestation or reactions in daily life situations. That's the essential. This essential you already have in your hands.

Chapter four

"Know who you are and there is nothing what can stop you."

YOU ARE SUCCESS

You are the success is the name of this book and it is also your primary manifestation possibility. To better understand this, try to say something about yourself that does not contain the word "I". There are many languages in this world where it is possible to talk without using the word "I", but there are also many languages where it is without using "I-word" not possible. Think about it for a moment. How limiting are many languages.

Now, try to say something about yourself without using any attribute to you (me, my, etc.). You surely found that you did not have any language possibilities to talk like this. And that's exactly what this chapter is about, what this book is about and what this searching of success is about. It is indisputable that the search for success has a totally different meaning as it is attributed to it. For this reason, it is possible to talk about hard work without which success cannot be achieved. But you already know that I'm showing a different way of manifesting your success. This different way what I showing is the search for joy and ease, not hardness. Success has an unlimited number of forms, so it can be manifested in any way, anytime, anywhere and by anyone. That is a fact which you can see everywhere around you. In order not to go into the philosophical neverending concepts, let's look at the success from other angles of view.

- *How can success that is you and that is only intellectually understood, be truly experienced and manifested?*

Success is nothing new, nothing special, but if you felt lack of it, you were unhappy and unsatisfied. Since the success is you, what lack did you experienced? Think about it for a moment. This is why it is necessary to know and not just to think that you know. You have to get through this intellectual lack of success illusion. In order to eliminate this illusion of lack, you can help yourself by saying "I am a success". It's a great way to get started. At the moment of reaching the success, you are already able to make your own statements based on your reached experiences.

Many tend to believe that by understanding success they have eliminated all concepts of disharmony (unpleasant situations). This is a huge and dangerous mistake, which you can see daily around you. You've certainly heard about someone (or even you know someone) who has become successful, but for a variety of reasons he lost that success. It was exactly that reason – the false thinking of knowing what success was (perhaps pride, superiority, carelessness or fear could played their part).

Success and concepts of disharmony or unpleasant situations are separated from each other. Whether unpleasant situations will appear manifest is entirely dependent on the individual, on you.

The same goes for the other way around. Many tend to believe that by understanding success they create concepts.

Success is the result of all possibilities, which was in the potential state. Success cannot be weighed or measured. Weighing and measuring is only possible with specific requirements. Success is freedom, success is joy, success is harmony of current moment and success is everything with which you are satisfied. For this reason, success can be customized at anytime, anywhere and by anyone. Success can be adapted to any needs at the current moment. That's the fact and best news in the same time.

If you gave to a word "success" (not the concept of success) attribute of importance, it manifested itself as a dual system of remuneration and punishment. From that moment it take the role either of the liberation, or the role of limitation. Both, liberation and limitation are the expression of fear of lack. Once you know it, you have a huge advantage over unexpected, undesired and unpleasant situations. Recognize them in time. Even the statement "I am a success" can be limiting as long as it is meant to achieve one option out of many. For this reason, as I have in this book mentioned, never give to anything extra significance. Let all things be what they really are.

-   With what kind of job can be success achieved if you know, that success is you?

From indefiniteness itself, success arises as a prerequisite for the manifestation of all your possibilities in a relative state. Stop to do all the work that forces you to create differences – both thought and material. Many teachings teach you to be different. I encourage and invite my clients and friends to be unique. This is a big and fundamental difference. Once you recognize your uniqueness, you become extremely interesting for whole business environments and the universe itself. Your uniqueness can be for many people seen as a difference and from this knowledge (that the other people seen you as a "difference") you can draw endless power of success. If you were only focusing on the difference, you would only be distanced from the outer world. Worse than that, you would be distanced from yourself, which is manifested as all the failures and all those undesirable or unpleasant situations. It is logical. You already know that there is no difference between us, between outer world and inner world. So what difference should we talk about? If everything is one, just be aware of the uniqueness which resides in yourself and which is you and become the most desirable recipient and giver of well-being.

What kind of job is the best? From all the existing jobs, there is only one which the best. It is the devotion to yourself, because it is also an amazing way of constant realizing your uniqueness.

- How do you achieve the details or concrete manifes-
tations of wanted and desired success if you already
know that success is you?

There is one process called impartiality. Impartiality is the real essence of manifesting anything you can imagine. You have often been literally said persecuted by the illusoriness of the relativity of success, which only strengthens your mistrust in yourself and to the running of things around you. The idea or concept taken from someone else is the illusion itself. This is the process in which you created your fictive borders and how you became unconscious slaves of someone else. Impartiality is the medicine for the undesired and unpleasant past situations. Impartiality gives you tremendous power to manifest. Impartiality gives you the ability to distinguish and see life situations as they really are.

- So how is it with that success?

Despite your day-to-day activities, you are absolutely free beings. You are the freedom yourself and no one can ever separate or to steal it from you. One of my friends and teachers, Viliam Horváth (†2017), said to me "Everything you have and what no one can ever steal from you is the wondrous and miraculous force of your mind." At this moment, these "mysterious" forces have become a real enrichment for me. Why am I writing about it? Because these wondrous and miraculous forces are also called "success". Are you able and willing to accept this statement?

Your success lies in the ability to recognize your uniqueness and to realize that you are the creator at any time, in every place and with the presence of every being. This is your greatest success – the success that you are. Of course, you can still become more and more and more successful, there is no doubt about it, but you are already the success. From this point of understanding and recognition, go and create your well-being. This is a gentle point, make sure that you understand it clearly. When you said that "I am Success" was not before your current (health, business, personal, or other) success, then in fact you say only that your life experiences was not similar and unified to this current success. Your life experience with the intellectually limited "I" did not recognized the absence of illusion. In other words, all past undesirable and unpleasant situations have you experienced as an injustice toward yourself only on the basis of ignorance. If you integrate the physical body and the physical world around you into the success equation, you break the harmonious concept of it.

How would you answer if I asked you to describe yourself how you looked 300 years ago? The most common answer would probably be "I was not". Since time and space do not exist, it would rather be a relativistic expression accepted as a fact of limitation and attachment to the currently perceived time and space. Perhaps it would be a better to answer "I was not like what I am". In other words, in the words of success "What did your success look like 300 years ago?" The answer is "It was not the same successfulness as I am, but the success was, is and will be unchangeable present". Everyone has the same experience without exception. There was no feeling of indefiniteness and impartiality, there was only something concrete. With this concreteness, you have always begun your daily activities that have always been tied to the relativity of time and space, the relativity of success and failure, the relativity of happiness and unhappiness and so on. It was the endless process of creating, shaping and manifesting unexpected situations. Now, that process is at its end, because you already know.

I have one example for you how to be harmonious in the moments of "waking up" and "falling asleep" that taught me my Guru Brug Lu.

Example and practice one
Waking up
   1. Wake up earlier than standard.
For your personal development this point is extremely important. This is the rules breaking par excellence. In this way, knowingly and willingly, you change your habits of inability to manage your successfulness. You can set your alarm clock, for example, one minute sooner as standard and in this way shorten the waking up time week to week. You can do so as long as it is comfortable for you, or until the moment of your desired successfulness occurred.

2. Wake up in silence or with calm music

Calm music should be a peaceful traditional music as Mantras or classical music are. If you wish to wake up with Mantra, is should be Mantra singed with real Monks. That is very important. Everyone who reproduces the Mantras of Monks puts in them (knowingly or unknowingly) his own limitations. You certainly don't want to make the mistake at the beginning of your journey that you become a slave to someone else's borders of ignorance. All tones outside the frequency of peace and silence cause far-reaching assumptions of distraction. The more music is closer to peace and silence, the more it enriches you.

Here is again what I often repeat "The most important is to know and not just thinking that you know."

3. When you are awake, don't think about what was in past and what will or should be in this day or in relative future. Just feel comfortable in your bed for a while.

Comfortable awakening is the basic of pure mind. In this pure minded way you attract clarity. In this state of clarity, you are able to recognize all the situations that can help you to have everything you want.

4. Make the first move slowly and sit quietly.

From not only the neurophysiological point of view, it is important to make your first move slowly. Slow motion is a drive for the harmonious functioning of your entire body. Length of sitting doesn't play any role here. Just enjoy this position.

5. Open your eyes with smile

Keep smiling is not just a blank motivational slogan. Smile is an immediate confirmation of satisfaction with the current moment (situation). This simplest mimic gesture can do and do miracles. With smile you should also work during the day. From the moment of waking up, practice it during whole day in any beginning and ending of situation and you will see how the day is changed immediately.

Example and practice two
Falling asleep

1. *Three hours before sleep don't eat and drink only an adequate amount of water (don't be overfilled).*

Understanding "good eating" habits is one of the conditions for achieving constant successfulness. Remember how you felt physiologically and mentally in the past when you ate too much, or you ate something very hard to digest. It wasn't so good. And that's exactly why "good eating" habits are so important. On the other hand, what you eat is reflected in how you think.

2. *Take low warm bath or shower short before sleep.*

Low warm bath or shower before sleeping soothes all the unnecessary elements of your body. Water is a programmable element and itself is an amazing cleanser for your body and mind. By working with water, I have experienced very interesting situations with myself, my clients and my friends, that have denied all physical laws. Water deserves special respect.

3. *Use simple Meditative techniques of retrospection before sleep.*

Meditation has become a modern phenomenon, but it also implies many misinterpretations. Meditation for financial or other profit is as absurd as sitting in a car and trying with him to cross the ocean. Meditation is not a closing eyes act. Meditation is a concrete quality of your life and it happen naturally. To meditate means that you have cultivated your whole system of being. This is why I say that you should use meditative techniques and not that you should meditate. Just take a relaxing position, in your own way and make retrospection of the day. Take all the best things from the day and if there was something you didn't like, leave it where it was, but outside of you. Use gratitude for the gifts of successfulness. If there was a lot of unpleasant situations, use gratitude for the gift of living, breathing or something other. Everyday there is something you can be grateful for.

4. *Shortly before sleep, leave all thoughts, people, situations, comfort of your bed and room, etc.*

This is the stage of liberating yourself from all the disturbing effects of the day. Of course, on the beginning of the practice the thoughts was coming and going. This is naturally state for thinking and that's absolutely all right. Leave them where they are, don't fight them. If you fought them, you only gave them the strength and thus you gave yourselves into a neverending circle of disharmony.

If you feel really tired and burdened with thoughts, use concentration technique on your breath. Breathe a little slowly and smoothly. Just breathe and relax. This is helping you to become a good and refreshing sleep.

5. *During sleep be in absolutely darkness, or have a lighted up an oil lamp.*

I used lighted oil lamp. The reason is that the combination of water (already described bath or shower) and fire immediately causes positive changes in your mindset. This method has been used in many cultures for thousands of years and is an excellent helper in achieving your desired successfulness.

There are many other techniques you can incorporate into your waking up and falling asleep system. Choose the ones that are best felt for you. In the waking up and falling asleep system is hiding a huge power.

At the beginning of all your successfulness was observation. Observing relativity and diversity of successful stories allows you to decide whether to accept or reject a given object or situation. You, as success itself, are here even when the relative successfulness was not present. Most of your goals are tied to physical expression (physical health, money, house, car, family and friends, etc.). For this reason, they are subject to finality. But you are not a thing, you are a manifestation of a human being.

There are no definitions, all this seeing is just your manifestation to yourself. That's why you are the success itself.

What I wanted to clarify here is that the greatest miracle is your constant manifestation of yourself – everything you think about and also everything you observe. It's your naturalness.

- *How to live constantly in the "golden day of excellence"?*

The golden day of excellence is a continuous life in well-being. You can convince yourself of the reality of this statement. Imagine for a short while that you hold in your hands such a powerful artifact, which allows you to be constantly in the right time, at the right place and with the right beings. What is the feeling? Definitely interesting. Did you know that such an artifact exist and its name is knowledge? Yes, this artifact is the knowledge you have at your disposal at any time, in every place and with the presence of every being. How's the feeling now when you know it? Is it interesting?

You have to know also, that knowledge requires one special behavior. You must immediately leave your pride of knowing success. If you know something, it's great, but it does not mean you should be full of pride of knowing it. Rejoice in your knowledge, beware of your knowledge, acknowledge your knowledge, but never be full of pride of knowing. Knowledge cannot speak, but this conversation relates only and absolutely to him. This conversation is a revelation and big enrichment of your current manifested knowledge.

You are already the success, therefore the success cannot be achieved. If you are already a human being, how more can you become a human being? It does not have a logic. If you are already the success and therefore the success cannot be achieved, what else can be achieved? You can be still more and more and more successful.

The following structure is helping you to be immediately in a state of successfulness. It is my absolutely favorite tool, which taught me by my Guru Brug Lu, for establishing an immediate and timeless harmony of successfulness.

Example

-   *Talk only about what you have a personal experience with*

If you look around yourself and think a little about what many people was saying, you have to be surprised. Many had a constant need to describe the diversity of existence. They described all kind of attributes of the gods, archangels, angels, spirits, souls and other various beings, they described physical and other mechanisms or laws, they commented on the old sacred texts and not anymore existing cultures, etc. Did they have a personal experience with it? Think about it for a moment. This is exactly what it is necessary to establish among your main priorities. Talking just about what you have a personal experience with. If you are talking about something you do not have experience with, you are creating a specific information space. This information space is freely manipulable, but its essence is ignorance and false belief. This must be avoided.

If you don't have your own personal experience, don't believe and don't disbelieve. If you need to discuss or comment on something you do not have a personal experience with, start with the self-questioning, because as you already know, you are the answer, you are the manifestation of everything.

- *Allow your mind to manifest itself and do all your actions in harmony with it*

Make it a habit to think that all of your mental and physical actions are done for the joyful benefit of yourself and others. Within this inner state you hold the highest pride (not the ego-pride) of being the holder of the main mind. Within this inner state you proclaim the intention to do joyful benefit for yourself and others. You are now within the mental and physical activity of union arising from placing your intention into the whole universe. This brings your main mind to the moment of successfulness. Cultivate your aspiration to attain successfulness for the joyful benefit of yourself and all beings and support this great intention as a loving parents cares for their child.

- *Focus on that you are, instead of that you must to have*

By focusing on the fact that you are, you are entering a space in which the abundance of everything continually flows. Your life is a process of being, not a process of achieving distant situations or goals. Therefore leave the idea of to have and to achieve. There is no destination between you, success and your successfulness.

You are is always more than to must have.

- Rejoice

Rejoicing from the achievement is a wonderful and powerful way of gratitude. It is fuel for an overall positive living approach to reaching everything desired. Rejoice in the possibility and opportunity to rejoice. That's the greatest rejoice. Rejoice in knowledge, joy, peace, harmony, happiness, health, wealth, beauty and all the abilities and possibilities manifested by you and all beings. Whenever you rejoice, you confirm and thus multiply all the positive possibilities of your manifestation in their potential state. It's like finding gold in a sediments of river. This makes joy of others also be your joy. Everything you rejoice is multiplied. Since there are so many beings, you can imagine how much fuel of positiveness and clearness you collect. If you already know this and if you've already felt the greatness of this incredible process, you will want for sure to practice rejoicing all day long. The most exciting thing about this incredible process is that you do not need to prepare yourself, to go anywhere, to buy anything and do not even have to search for any teacher. You can do this anytime. In this way the boundaries of time and space that stood between you and your wanted, desired and expected successfulness literally break. Do you want to accumulate any kind of wealth without doing anything? Do you want to be quick successful? My answer is "Just rejoice". If you see or hear that someone was doing a good and positive process, rejoice in that process and you accumulate all that beautiful work done. Nothing more, nothing less.

-   Give and take

Give and take, or send and receive is a beautiful technique for achieving a harmony of successfulness. In this technique you can visualize the relativity of suffering of yourself or others on the inhale and on the exhale you are giving joyfulness and successfulness to yourself and all beings.

Here, it is extremely important to realize that you should not to be identified either with failure or with successfulness. Simply visualize the previously seen status. If you identify yourself with something, you can manifest unwanted, undesirable and unpleasant situations. Just do it easily and with joy.

-   Recite your statements regularly

Reciting and repetitions have their communication meaning of manifestation in its potential state. You should have your own statements, but you can use any statement, in which you feel to "be at home". My clients and friends have greatly appreciated my statements which I (some of them) present to you with joy.

"Let the eternal abundance be preserved and manifested by my being."

"Let the great increasing of abundance still flowing through my whole being."

"Let the splendid abundance is in my all manifestations."

The previous structure is helping you be immediately in a state of successfulness. The golden day of excellence is absolutely in your hands as all your manifestations. Just have in your mind the process behind indescribableness and inexpressibleness. In every moment you are practices in the base of miraculous powers of your essence based on intention with the abilities to immediately abandoning all the unpleasant situations. You know how it was to be in isolation or boundaries and you know how it was to be free from isolation or boundaries. You know also how the incredible process of transformation works, so go and take what you wanted and desired manifestations to your golden days of excellence.

- *Is there another angle of view of manifesting what you want?*

There is a theme that clarifies many details of your all-round successfulness journey. This theme is to understand the process of allowing. The only need of your current moment is to fill the space between who you were and who you allow yourself to be. This theme has nothing to do with social or other responsibility. It is the theme of ease and difference in communication skills. I have written enough about the communication skills, but there is one more level of communication skills you should know about. This level is the difference between using statements as "it is", "we are" and "I am".

In your daily experience exist a specific trigger or confirmation for concrete manifestations. This trigger or confirmation is the using of three word-connections. They are:

- *"It is"* as the most powerful trigger or confirmation for all manifestations in potential state in the timelessness
- *"We are"* as the most powerful trigger or confirmation for all manifestations in the direction from timelessness to the current time and space
- *"I am"* as the most powerful trigger or confirmation for beginning and for the ending of all manifestations in the current time and space

For a better understanding, I give you the following examples for all three word-connections.

Example one "IT IS"

IT IS

(The most powerful trigger or confirmation for all manifestations in potential state in the timelessness)

The "it is" follows indescribableness as a help in attracting the right successful manifestations. If someone said "it is impossible", followed all kind of circumstances supporting that negative confirmation statement and the unpleasant situation was occurred. If someone said "it is great", followed all kind of circumstances supporting that positive confirmation statement and the pleasant situation was occurred.

Therefore the word-combination "it is" should be used in present time and with some powerful statement. By description of **awareness of "bad habits"**, I showed you the refinement transformation possibilities. That was not the same theme as this theme about word-connections, even though they may appear to be the same or similar. The difference is in the main process. In the refining process, you get the desired refinement effect of manifestation from an already existing unwanted, undesirable and unpleasant situation, while by using simple word-connections is to use them correctly in the right time, at the right place and for the right beings to attract the right successful manifestations with absolute primary simplicity. This means avoiding the unwanted, undesirable and unpleasant situation before it manifests.

There are 12 basic ways to use "it is" correctly in the right time, at the right place and provided to the right beings. I invite you to use this great creation and manifestation process which is in its potential state.

I.   *Unknown using of "it is"*

In this form is the "it is" in unknown state, which you cannot describe. If you cannot describe it, use it as simple as you can. Here belongs all the situations you did not have a personal experience with.

Statement
"It is as it is."

II.   Known using of "it is"

In this form is the "it is" in knowing and therefore dynamic state, which you can in some way describe. Its dynamism comes from its association with all possible manifestations in the potential state. It is a reflection of them. Here occurs the first time the concept of duality – unknown and known. Here belongs all dynamic situations.

Statement
"It is as best as it is."

III.   Universal using of "it is"

In this form is the "it is" in universal personalized mani-festation. In this state is it the creative factor or power or force and the source of everything what you will think, what you will talk and what you will act. Here belongs all situations connected with the relativity of time and space. At this moment, you have become the creator and bearer of the relativity of time and space.

Statement
"It is as greatest as it was and as it can be."

IV.   Identifiable using of "it is"

In this form is the "it is" in identifiable state as a progres-sive projection. In this state is it the first manifestation, which is both distinct (all your conscious thoughts, words and acts) and indistinct (all your unconscious thoughts, words and acts). This state includes all the so-called life examinations. All your thoughts, words and acts become a living beings. Simply to say, you are the only teacher of yourself. It seems everything as a philosophy concept, but thing about it for a moment. It have its logic and it is very important to understand it.

Statement

"It is a greatest manifestation."

V. Manifested or physical using of "it is"

In this form is the "it is" in the state of all your physical senses. In this state occurs first tangible or material materialization. This materialization took place on the basis of the alignment of all your previous thoughts, words and acts in cooperation with all the possibilities of time and space relativity.

Statement

"It is a greatest materialization."

VI. Personal using of "it is"

In this form is the "it is" in the individual or personal state with all possible qualities. In this state occurs the existence that you know. This existence took place on the basis of all creation processes, both known and unknown. This existence is the result of your constant process of developing from the relative satisfaction to the absolute satisfaction. It is a process of self-comprehension and not self-correction. It is important to realize this.

Statement

"It is a greatest being."

VII. Time committed using of "it is"

In this form is the "it is" in the state of time committing as the beginning and the ending possibilities. In this state occurs the whole concept of time. You need to know, that only your physical manifestation can be "ruled" with the concept of time. Everything else is timeless. In this state you are the ruler of the time, so use it wisely.

Statement
"It is a greatest beginning and ending."

VIII. Uniqueness using of "it is"

In this form is the "it is" in the unique state of all creative concepts. In this state occurs the whole concept of creation and it is needed to work as a unity. That means, that your thoughts, words and acts must be in harmony – in unity as one and only concept.

Statement
"It is a greatest uniqueness."

IX. Space committed using of "it is"

In this form is the "it is" in the state of space committing as the power behind expression. In this state occurs the whole concept of space. The space acts as the mediator between all powers and manifestations in you and in the whole universe. The sound of your speech let all your inner powers pass through the space. This is how you transform the world and universe around you. That's why I often invite my clients and friends to keep an eye on what they are talking about. This kind of space can expand end-lessly, therefore you can be what you want to be and have what you want to have. In this state you are the ruler of the space, so use it wisely.

Statement
"It is a greatest universe."

X.   Specific word-form using of "it is"
In this form is the "it is" in the state of specific word-form as the power behind all communication possibilities. In this state occurs the whole concept of speech. This is the origin of everything. To be able to achieve and be in this state, you must use only the right and needed words, in the right time, at the right place and provided to the right be-ings. What are the right words? These are all the words that are spoken only on the basis of your own experience, provided in the right time, at the right place and to the right beings.

Statement
"It is a greatest speech."

XI.   Food committed using of "it is"
In this form is the "it is" in the state of nourishment as the power behind all food – mental and physiological. In this state occurs the whole concept of information nourish-ment. Here you create all the information values not only for yourself but for all beings and the universe as one. Based on these information values, all manifestations are

occurred in the current time and space and in the potential state. These states are only gained by the concrete importance, which you have assigned them. The more importance, the higher the possibility of manifestation.

Therefore, it is very important to pay attention to the nourishment you receive.

Statement
"It is a greatest nourishment."

XII.   The very using of "it is"

In this form is the "it is" in the unconditioned state as the part of yourself. In this state is it without ending. It is a state of essence of things that does not depend on others, it is an inner nature. Here you create replicas for yourself, therefore it is extremely important to know yourself, to know, that you are. If you have knowing about yourself, your mind is not anymore attached to the outside stimuli or moods, but is filled with self-control and self-contained. Peace, harmony, wisdom, mind, senses and body are your beautiful helpers, which you carry still with you. The true state of very using of "it is" is pure, real and blissful. You have to also now, that the bliss is the essential nature of you and that there is no difference between you and bliss, because you are blissful. Any possibility that is true, real, eternal and undeniable, and whose essence is unchanging is termed as "yourself".

Statement
"It is a greatest bliss."

249

Example two "WE ARE"

WE ARE

(The most powerful trigger or confirmation for all manifestations in
the direction from timelessness to the current time and space)

The "we are" follows the most powerful trigger or confirmation for all manifestations in potential state in the timelessness as a help in attracting the right successful manifestations. If someone used "we are" in a standard way, followed all kind of circumstances supporting that standard confirmation statement and all the unpleasant situation was occurred. If you were using the "we are" in a standard way, you only confirmed the specific multiplication fact (plural in the direction of many). Your mind has received such information values as a passive state of disinterest and leaving you flowing at the waves of the majority. Such a condition was similar to intoxication and during this intoxication state was manifested all possible scenarios often described as an unpleasant situations.

If someone used "we are" with the knowledge that "he is them" and "they are him", followed all kind of circumstances supporting that powerful uniqueness confirmation statement and the miraculous situation was occurred. If you were using the "we are" with the knowledge that "you are they" and "they are you", your mind has accepted it as a relaxing active stimulus for creation. At this time, all manifestations in the potential state are for you available and you can handle them at your best discretion.

Therefore, anyone who wants to make an absolute change of their life (mental and physical) patterns, instead of standard expressions such as "I am" and "we are (plural in the direction of many)", should use only the concept of "we are" in its true meaning values in the right time, at the right place and provided to the right beings.

The concept "we are" is much more peaceful, enjoyable, emotional and relaxing statement than any other statement or word-connection.

There are 12 basic ways to use "we are" correctly in the right time, at the right place and provided to the right beings. I invite you to use this great creation and manifestation process which is in the direction from timelessness to the current time and space.

I.   Using of "we are" as a concept of knowledge

In this form is the "we are" in the state of knowledge as the power behind all knowing. This is freely available state to everyone. This is a kind of real knowledge that is unique to your Consciousness. It is not related to your intellectual kind of describing as the thoughts, words, desires, beliefs, learning theories, promises and any other individual or group of your concepts. This kind of knowledge is the great self-created and self-renewed space or void between. You must understand that this knowledge is still and everywhere with you.

Statement
"We are a greatest knowledge."

251

II.   Harmonious using of "we are"

In this form is the "we are" in the state of harmony as the equalizing power. In this state is it the pure information value. There is a big need to be in harmony within yourself and also with other beings. What kept you in disharmony? Observation of yourself, others, the world and the universe to which you gave some importance.

Let all your observations be in the state of the reality, peace, patience and harmony and let them be in accordance with all beings.

Statement
"We are a greatest harmony."

III.   Experienced using of "we are"

In this form is the "we are" in the state of experience as the ability to meditate. In this state is it the fuel of all experiences. The ability to meditate is fuel alone which gives you all the relative hidden powers or energies of universe. The ability to meditate gives you the opportunity to use your full potential and thus to gain the necessary experience needed to manifest everything you want. There are three steps to proceed as follows:

- recognize and get to know the power or energy;
- acquire and learn how to work with that power or energy;
- direct and use that power or energy in the right way;

Statement
"We are a greatest experience."

IV.   Using of "we are" as a concept of providing
In this form is the "we are" in the state of providing as the understanding to seek "security". In this state is it as a patience in providing information values leading to security satisfaction. As you can see, this is not the social meaning of security, this is the security, which is more as a satisfaction. Why is that? Think about that for a moment. What is behind the word "security"? Searching to be secure, is to search to be satisfied with all information values. And this is exactly the reason why the state of providing specific information values constantly occur.

You have to be able to share merits, good will and the honest teachings to all beings who are able to hear and see (not only physiological), regardless of the disturbance by their egos.

Statement
"We are a greatest messengers."

V.   Prosperous using of "we are"
In this form is the "we are" in the state of prosperity as the inner and outer strength, will power and desire, geniality, famousness, virtues and concrete identifiable multidimensional character. In this state is it as an all wealth aspect of the world and universe.

Statement
"We are a greatest blessed abundance of wealth and prosperity."

VI.   Radiant using of "we are"

In this form is the "we are" in the state of blissful and loving radiation as the essence of beginning. In this state is it as a visualized possibility. Your change is a change for others and that is the exact meaning of the blissful and loving radiation process. All the manifested changes provided to other beings are the possibility and ability to transform all kinds of matter.

Before all the beginnings (thoughts, words and actions), the essence of the beginning is manifested and that manifestation is the blissful and loving radiation.

Statement

"We are a greatest blissful radiation."

VII.   Conquer using of "we are"

In this form is the "we are" in the state of conquering as the power of change and separation. In this state is it the power of transformation. This state gives you the power of transforming everything you want for the needs of conquer all unwanted, undesirable and unpleasant situations. As you can see, also here it is not the social meaning of something to "conquer". It is the possibility to change and separate with peace and harmony all the unwanted, undesirable and unpleasant situations and thus awaken all your infinite possibilities.

Statement

"We are a greatest conqueror."

VIII.   Beautiful using of "we are"

In this form is the "we are" in the wonderful state of beauty as the power of art. In this state is it a loving possibility of singular longing. This singular longing is the art of living. The art of living lies in its simplicity, which is at the same time also the fuel for all your transformational processes in potential state. Just be simple in your thoughts, words and actions and create beauty all around you. Yes, you have to create beauty all around you in the name of love and truth. Be still joyful with your loving manifestations.

Statement

"We are a greatest beauty."

IX.   Healthy using of "we are"

In this form is the "we are" in the state of health as the power of medicine. In this state is it in as the two possibilities – health and health in potential state. One of the most used words in the world was a disease. This status is necessary to understand. An explanation of the social concept of disease is as follows. The disease is nothing but health in a potential state. For this reason, it is necessary to look at each state of your mental and physical manifestation as a condition in potential state. Health is a general state of well-being and everything else is only a relative and temporary departure from this reality.

Statement

"We are a greatest health."

X.   Functional using of "we are"

In this form is the "we are" in the functional state as the power of result. In this state is it as the harmonious manifestation of all past decisions. Functionality is an indication of correctness of your thoughts, words and actions patterns. The state of functionality is a state of eternity and the information value of this functionality is portable to any being in the right time and at the right place. It is enough that one is ready receive it. Applying this process you can see in all the successes around you. Behind every success was "hidden" this process.

Statement
"We are a greatest evidence of functionality."

XI.   Preservation using of "we are"

In this form is the "we are" in the state of informational preservation as the power of continuation. In this state is it most valuable information. What is most valuable information? Wasting of your life energy brings you only unsuccessfulness, while the maintenance of your life energy brings absolute and unconditional successfulness. The informational preservation is extremely necessary to continuation of all beings and the whole universe. Only with the maintenance of your life energy you are able to be successful in any way.

Statement
"We are a greatest preservation."

XII.   Concealment using of "we are"

In this form is the "we are" in the concealment state as the power behind seeing things as they really are. In this state is it the ability to be conscious free from all failures. What is to be hidden here and why should be that hidden? All the negative, unwanted, undesirable and unpleasant situations. You should never talk or write about your negative experiences only so! Never ever! The more communication (unmanifested and manifested) was negative, the more negative situations was attracted. The more people were dragged into this negative process, the more people were affected. It was a big circle of unwanted, undesired and unpleasant situations. Keep in mind that where there are no questions, there are no answers. But also applies where the questions are, it is necessary to provide the right answers in the right time, at the right place and to the right beings. Also remember that you have to spread beauty and not sadness.

Find a way to provide beautiful information values for even the most severely felt life situations. If you can do this, you can create and manifest anything you want. And that's the exact meaning of concealment.

As a conscientist, you are knowingly concealing the negativity to others in order to preserve beauty. By doing that, you let others see things as they really are. This is an amazing job which brings immediate miracles.

Statement
"We are a greatest concealment."

Example three "I AM"

I AM

(The most powerful trigger or confirmation for beginning and for the
ending of all manifestations in the current time and space)

The "I am" follows the most powerful trigger or confirmation for all manifestations in the direction from timelessness to the current time and space as a help in attracting the right successful manifestations.

If someone used "I am" in a standard way, followed all kind of circumstances supporting that standard confirmation statement and all the unpleasant egocentric oriented situation was occurred. If you were using the "I am" in a standard way, you only confirmed the specific multiplication fact of egocentric expression. Your mind has received such information values as an active state of disinterest for others (also for the world and universe itself) and leaving you flowing at the waves of egocentric ignorance. Such a condition was similar to state of aggression and during this aggression state was manifested all possible violent scenarios often described as an extra challenging unpleasant situations.

If someone used "I am" with the knowledge that this word combination is the ruler of beginning and ending for all manifestations in the current time and space (how the manifestations are), followed all kind of circumstances supporting that powerful uniqueness confirmation statement and the wanted and desired manifestations occurred. If you were using the "I am" with the knowledge like that, your mind has accepted it as a natural nonviolent command for creation and manifestation. At this time, all manifestations in the potential state are ready to manifest in the best possible way for you.

Therefore, anyone who wants to make an big and immediate change of their life (mental and physical) patterns, instead of standard social expressions "I am", should use only the concept of "I am" in its true meaning values in the right time, at the right place and provided to the right beings. The "I am" is not about yourself, it is about confirmation, because it is a power behind manifestations depended on time and space. It is not your social personality concept, it is the (till today) not correct described (by modern physics and philosophers) energy concept, which creates the difference between all the possibilities of manifestation. You used this concept in the unconscious way every moment, but in this moment is it for you already a well-known concept ("revealed"). Therefore you are able to use it in a conscious and precise directed way.

How to use them? Before each use of the word-connection "I am", note that you do not talk about yourself, but that you use the power of specific or sublime energy in accordance to create in the current time and space.

The concept "I am" is much more lovingly directive statement than any other statement or word-connection.

There are 12 ways to use "I am" correctly in the right time, at the right place and provided to the right beings. I invite you to use this great creation, confirmation and manifestation process which is here for beginning and for the ending of all manifestations in the current time and space.

I.   *Using of "I am" as a concept of beginning*
In this form is the "I am" in the state of beginning as the power behind all manifestations in potential state. This is natural state to everyone. This state is also your protective space with all the options for repair (if is needed).
You know really well that at the beginning of all your activities there were many undesirable questions, such as "Can I do that?", "How can I do it best way?", "Where to find it?", "Will I recover?", "Will this person become my partner?", "Is it possible to be successful?" and so on. At this moment, all powers and protective mechanisms in potential state are grouped together. If you wish to achieve the wanted and desired manifestation, you must direct them before all your "I am" thought, words and actions in a conscious way.
Before each use of the word-connection "I am", note that you do not talk about yourself, but that you use the power of specific or sublime energy in accordance to create in the current time and space.

Statement
"I am a greatest order."

II.   Wise using of "I am"

In this form is the "I am" in the state of wisdom as the all-knowing intelligence potential. In this state is it a reviving system of choice. You can name it also as an intuitive wisdom or understanding. This state is a kind of knowledge or understanding that is beyond your mind and beyond your social intellect, which provides vision and guidance, to all the other concepts of "I am".

How to practice it? It can be experienced only in the absence of the social "I-ness". That means, your mind must be in a stable place without all the questionings. Only so you can experience the peace and silence needed to run the power of "I am". The true experience with all-knowing intelligence potential recognizes their own indescribableness and also recognizes that the only true experience is the manifested being itself, who is not the social "I".

Statement
"I am a greatest knowledge."

III.   Concentrative using of "I am"

In this form is the "I am" in the state of concentration as the power to grow. In this state is it the conscious knowing status of absorbing all the past information values directly activated. This is the concentration itself oriented on the single manifestation as an automatic growing process.

Statement
"I am a greatest concentration."

IV.   Diligent using of "I am"

In this form is the "I am" in the state of diligence as the power of achieving. In this state is it as the activity itself. This is the attitude of thankfully and gladly engaging in all kind of activities and functions to cause you to complete all the wanted and desired manifestations.

This is a state of enormous life power and energy, when you know you can be whatever you want, you can do whatever you want and you can achieve whatever you want for yourself and others. Let your intention be constantly active, persistent, undisturbed by anything from outside or from inside, unrelated to the relativity of time and space, ignoring the circumstances of the relative manifestations and reviving everything wonderful. Let it be aware of the positiveness, beauty, freedom and joy.

Statement

"I am a greatest potential."

V.   Patient using of "I am"

In this form is the "I am" in the state of patience as the power of forgiveness. In this state is it as the interpersonal practice of perfection. It is the ability of manifesting patience toward all kind of situations, both pleasant and unpleasant. You have often acted unworthy and impatient, which is at this moment just a relative past information value which you can transform in the best way. Now you have a conscious choice to apply patience as a peaceful and joyful gift, rather than a state of sadness and depression in which many felt the need to act in unwanted, undesirable and unpleasant way.

First of all (in this state), forgive yourself, but it shouldn't be neither through fear nor weakness. From all the intentions that lead into your freedom, joyfulness, successfulness and satisfaction, none is better than real and honest patience.

Statement

"I am a greatest gift of patience."

VI.   Discipline using of "I am"

In this form is the "I am" in the state of discipline as the power of be in the right time, at the right place and with the right beings. In this state is it the ability to constantly flow. Discipline is the whole process of naturalness to be in harmony with the most important option until its transformation, manifestation and materialization.

The discipline contains three states as it manifests itself:

- Consciousness in choosing the right transformation, manifestation and materialization;
- Anchoring the correctness of the selection;
- Controlling the process until it materializes;

Bring benefit to all beings with your intentions and once the time has come for you to do so, you must be free from any selfish motivations.

Statement

"I am a greatest naturalness."

VII.   Generous using of "I am"

In this form is the "I am" in the state of generosity as the power of giving and sharing. In this state is it the analogical respect for all beings, manifestations and materializations in the world and universe. That means, if you give an example of yourself, you give the whole protection, if you give smile, you give life energy, if you give food, you give possibility to live in another way, if you give something material, you strengthen physical possibilities, etc. However, have still in your mind, that this process must be in harmony with the right time, space and beings or situations. Honest, conscious, free from expectation and correctly done generosity helps to achieve everything.

Statement

"I am a greatest gift."

VIII.   Excellent using of "I am"

In this form is the "I am" in the state of excellence as the power of motivation and application. In this state is it present as the whole process of seeing things from another angle of view. To be excellent is to be focused on difference. I often received such a questions:

"What should I do to get what I want?"

My answer was always the same and with the same amazing successful result:

"By that question you have created the premise for your successfulness. Therefore, just act differently than usually."

The "secret" process of seeing things from another angle of view is very interesting possibility you still carry within yourself. Keep in mind that a non-standard behavior patterns are often a huge option and a starting point to go out from the unwanted, undesirable and unpleasant situation.

Statement

"I am a greatest excellence."

IX.   Truthful using of "I am"

In this form is the "I am" in the state of truthfulness as the power of reality. In this state is it as the whole communication process, both unmanifested and manifested. This is not a social description of the seen and felt values, this is the true essence of everything. How can you achieve this kind of knowing? By leaving the "I" concept.

Statement

"I am a greatest truth."

X.   Determinational using of "I am"

In this form is the "I am" in the state of determination as the power of resolve to become. In this state is it as an act of coming to a concrete decision in accordance to manifest and materialize wanted and desired successfulness.

Determination is not time and space bound. You have already determined and everything you live is the result of your determination. Think about it.

Statement

"I am a greatest decision."

XI.   Equanimity using of "I am"

In this form is the "I am" in the state of equanimity as the power of cultivation. In this state is it the quality of yourself as you are. At this point, you have to be especially aware of that, regardless of the mental or physiological condition you were in, you are always in harmony as the human being. If you were not, then you would not be manifested and materialized at all.

How you can be conscious in the state of equanimity and so strengthen it? Be merciful, compassionate, joyful and free with yourself and all beings. This is the way you can cultivate yourself, others and space around you.

Statement
"I am a greatest cultivation."

XII.   Using of "I am" as a concept of ending

In this form is the "I am" in the state of ending as the power behind all finalized manifestations which are still in potential state. This is natural state of everyone.

The final product is always an absolute expression of all past efforts. It is an absolute joy and happiness that contains all the knowledge about its origin. But ending is not the end itself. Ending or final product is always only enriching the whole. This is very important to be aware of.

As all the finalization options are included on the beginning, all possibilities of other relative beginnings are included in the ending. Therefore, it is never possible to achieve absolute successfulness. If you are already a success, what kind of success you want to achieve more? There are only countless options of successfulness that are constantly multiplied by your presence at a particular time, at a particular place and in the presence of particular beings. This is another reason why it is so easy to be successful. Just look at your patterns of beginnings and endings and you will (in current moment) see the amazing perspective of the options they offer you. In the moments of that amazing joyfulness when you have reached your wanted and desired successfulness, realize with all your "I am" ("I am successful businessman", "I have reached what I wanted", "I am cured", etc.) statements that it is not the end, but just another beginning of countless successful beginnings in the relative state. In that way of thinking and acting, you are able to be always in the state of joyful freedom of success which is you.

Statement
"I am a greatest result."

As you could see, in your daily experience exist a specific trigger or confirmation for concrete manifestations. You already know about them and you already see your success reality from another angle of view. Success is without a beginning or an ending, but successfulness possibilities which are manifested and materialized are ruled with the laws of a beginning or an ending. Therefore you can manipulate them as you like and be successful as much as you wish for. In order to have more practical possibilities of the above writing, I invite you to take a look at the triple opinion statements.

Example of 22 triple creation statements

I

It is as greatest as it can be
We are the magnificent greatestness for all beings
I am the fantastic greatestness for all times

II

It is as most wonderful to feel freedom as it can be
We are the most wonderful to feel freedom for all beings
I am the most wonderful to feel freedom each moment

III

It is as most blissful joyfulness as it can be
We are the most blissful joyfulness for all beings
I am the most blissful joyfulness in every situation

IV

It is as miraculous knowledge as it can be
We are an opened miraculous knowledge for all beings
I am the flowing miraculous knowledge in the whole life

V

It is as healthy to feel life as it can be
We are the most amazing medicine for all beings
I am a most joyful holder of blessed health

VI

It is an eternal source of abundance
We are the abundance of all being
I am the flowing abundance at this moment

VII

It is a union of everything in the whole universe
We are the beautiful unity of everything
I am the famous unity of all times

VIII

It is as harmonious as it can be
We are the peaceful harmony of everything
I am the celebration harmony of time

IX

It is the most famous, magnificent and miraculous birth
We are the blissful birth of everything
I am an eternal cycle of well-being

X

It is an awesome attraction of successfulness
We are the process and evidence of attracting all the
wanted and desired successfulness
I am the wanted and desired successfulness of all beings

XI

It is the dimension of peace, silence and freedom itself
We are the peace, silence and freedom for all beings
I am the peace, silence and freedom behind time

XII

It is as loving patience as it can be
We are a tolerant and forgiving manifestation of patience
I am the patience in every non-activity and activity

XIII

It is the most beautiful among all beautifulness
We are as beautiful as we can be
I am the beauty of time

XIV

It is the most amazing eternal love in all beings
We are the most joyful feel love between all beings
I am the love of the time of all lovers

XV

It is the greatest hope to be as it is
We are that miraculous hope that connects everything
with everything
I am the hope that liberate all beings from the boundaries

XVI

It is a nourishing understanding of all beings
We are the understanding that is gratifying to life
I am an understanding of the beauty to live the life

XVII

It is the power behind all the forces of creation
We are the power behind all materialized manifestations
I am the creative power of a successful progress

XVIII

It is the limitless nature of the whole creation
We are the limitless nature of the joy of all beings
I am the limitless nature of finality

XIX

It is a reviving gratitude for freedom
We are the reviving gratefulness of all beings
I am a reviving gratitude of all beginnings and endings

XX

It is the best of all possible thoughts, words and actions
We are the greatest and most beautiful result of all
thoughts, words and actions
I am at the beginning and ending of all thoughts, words
and actions

XXI

It is a fascinating and unique way of self-creating
We are a unique way of confirming the possibility of creating ourselves
I am a unique way towards the wanted and desired creation, manifestation and materialization of myself

XXII

It is the most astonishing physical creation, manifestation
and materialization in the whole universe
We are the physical creation, manifestation and materialization of beauty itself
I am a physical materialization of timelessness

271

You can build similar forms or statements of creation to support your successfulness at any time. You can built them in chronological order, but you can built them also in the accordance of you current need or impulse. It's your creation process, so give him sincere attention.

- ***What is the best job for you?***
There are a number of theories about this question which are based on either someone's personal experience or just a generalization of several theories. There are, of course, experts who are able to lead you to some kind of work that can satisfy you. These are all the facts you have every time available. I invite you to a process that is simple and in absolute harmony with yourself.
The main process of getting the best job
In the moment you start working with this process (you already started), you have to know that something like "the best job for me" does not exist. There are only endless pos-sibilities to multiply your past requirements.
If you are aware of this, answer the following questions that make up selection and choice from your past endless multiplied possibilities:

- If you like physical work, what makes you the most free and joyful on it?
- If you like mental work, what makes you the most free and joyful on it?

- If you like to work alone, what makes you the most free and joyful on it?
- If you like to work in a group, what makes you the most free and joyful on it?
- What makes you the most free and joyful about the results you have achieved on these questions (vision of money, vision to be famous, vision to be healthy, vision of another relationships, ability to have, ability to achieve, ability to control and so on)?

Now answer as quickly as possible:

- What is that what I want to do, what really irresistibly enchants and attracts me?
- Which three business areas are most attracted me?
- Which three places are most attracted me?

You've just gotten interesting and customized answers by yourself. Think peacefully above them. Now, when looking for "the right job", you need to be aware that your first intention should not be the money itself. Why? If is someone looking for something, he does so from a lack of it. Do not look for what you do not have in your hands, look for what is emotionally hidden behind the subject you are looking for. That's important to know. Are money bad intention? Definitely not! In order to make the perceived lack of money more refined and more ease, replace the word money with the word-connection financial freedom or well-being, or something that make you more enjoyable by working with this process. You need to be well in your daily life situations, you need to have fun and you need to have free and joyful feelings of everything you do, both mentally and physically. That is the foundation of your successfulness – freedom and joy.

In other hand of this process, the greatest possible form of achieving your wanted and desired job or successfulness is to remember how have you already achieved your successfulness. Just remember!

"Those who stayed intoxicated in the relationship with the relativity of their succeeding, they already lost their successfulness. Those who are in the state of understanding that they are the one and only success for themselves, are successful forever."

- ***What is the value of successfulness?***

In addition to the values set by separate economic systems, the true value of successfulness is generated only by yourself. What value did you assign to something, that was exactly what was it worth. You need to realize the true value of money or all-round successfulness. It is only a game of social imagination. Nothing else. If you accept it, you are a slave of current system, but if you understand the true values, you are free from all systems. There is a beautiful abundance that has no boundaries and that is constantly near you. Therefore, start with setting values based on the attractiveness of good feelings. You have to understand and know that you are looking for the values behind your wishes and desires, behind the relativity of successfulness. Do not care what the values are attributed by others to the same object. That's not your job. Your job is to be free with the best feelings in the right time, at the right place and with the right beings.

You already know, that the success is you and you also know, how to be successful. You already know, that there are no boundaries and you also know, that you did every time, everywhere and with everyone in the best way you knew. I invite you and urge you at the same time to use only the best-felt systems that let you be free in reaching whatever you want.

"It is necessary to restore your inner and outer order, therefore, act mentally and physically with humility. This is an awesome message and knowledge for you, because your wanted, wished and desired change is already on the way to you. Be attentive and helpful to all situations around you, because everything is ready to manifest and materialize. Your marvelousness is knocking on your door. Just go open it and create the absolute harmony which you deserve!"

Bonus chapter one

"The structure and origin of the success."

40 DAY SUCCESS

With big pleasure I introduce you this bonus chapter one,

which you can be seen as more detailed explanation of the described facts of the whole knowledge system that you are the success itself. "The 40 day success" system are representations of all the basic principles of your own reality, which provide you a big and powerful strategy of the conscious creating, manifesting and materializing everything you wish for.

As you could see, I really like to work with numerical and schematic systems. I connect everything what is relatively unconnectable, which guarantees my clients, my friends and now even to you all, be always in the state of ability to create. This "40 day success" system is no exception.

I created this "40 day success" system to regenerate your whole being and re-establish your natural essence, which is freedom, joy and all-round successfulness. This system is functional in time and space, but it is absolutely functional also outside of the relativity of time and space. This system is wherever you need it, because this system is your personal power and strength.

I invite you now to take part in this amazing and powerful "40 day success" journey, to become that you really are.

ay one

Main theme of the day

The power of materialization

The materialization is everything that you observed and lived in your daily life. It was you in current time and space. It was the result or completion of all your past thoughts, words and actions. Understand that what you considered to be your reality (whole materialization) was there only to show you all the possibilities how to achieve what you really wish for.

The main process of the day

Today, ignore your current materialized "reality" and focus only on what you really wish for. You cannot feel bad and in the same time achieve what you wish for! Either success ("good" or fortune or experiencing pleasant situations) or the relativity of success ("evil" or misfortune or experiencing unpleasant situations).

Today, describe one positive felt situation from your past, what kind of thoughts, words and actions could have materialized it.

Today, use miraculous power of the earth. Go into the nature and walk around there a while barefoot or do any activity during which you are connected with the earth.

Today's experience?

Day two

Main theme of the day

The power of connection

Connection is the space of your willpower. In that space is done only by your will as the materialization in your current reality, as it was created and manifested in your mind. It is a space which is beyond your mind. Imagination, motivation and intuition are the tools you need to have in your mind by working with that space. Therefore, your thoughts, feelings and willpower must be absolutely freed from your materialization.

The main process of the day

Today, use your imagination and motivation with most joyful thoughts and feelings, by searching only the best felt situations.

Today, use your honorable will and set the whole day be your best intuitive day.

Today, use miraculous power of the water. Go into the nature and swim or do any activity during which you are connected with the water.

Today's experience?

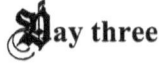ay three

Main theme of the day

The power of transformation

The transformation of this day is based on the triple component. This three component consists of your matter, energy and consciousness. They works together and are precisely what you call as the impressions.
Therefore, your impressions are an indicator of three component transformation (matter, energy and consciousness) in terms of creation.

The main process of the day

Today, use your impressions as a provider of the matter, energy and consciousness to make the situations happen.

Today, use self-reflection and a direct experience, to feel the indescribable life energy. Just feel and enjoy it.

Today, use miraculous power of the fire. Do any joyful, safe and legal activity during which you are for a while connected with possibility to handling with the fire (it's about the impression of the possibility ...of lighting a match or a candle, of lighting a fire in the fireplace, etc.).

Today's experience?

Day four

Main theme of the day

The power of transferability

The transferability is your amazing opportunity to be constantly helpful (to yourself and others). That means, that the transferability is a description of precise energy process, which filled the imaginary space in your creation processes. This energy acting based on necessity and logic, that is, on the basis of all your past decisions that led to a logical result or materialization.

Therefore, your decisions must be every time conscious.

The main process of the day

Today, use your decisions as a provider of the best possible transferable information value.

Today, use some way of transport from place to place and observe what everything was behind that process.

Today, use miraculous power of the air. Do any joyful activity in the nature, during which you are focused on your breathing. Just feel the connection and possibility to breathe (it's about the awareness of the possibility to feel the transferability process).

Today's experience?

ay five

Main theme of the day

The power of possibilities

The possibilities have their real place. That place is the most subtle level of whole matter, both materialized and in its potential state. From this place or space you created everything you see, everything you are.

When your natural possibilities (all your needs for life) was disturbed by negativity and ignorance, your mental and physiological patterns became enormous – you were in unpleasant situations.

Therefore, you must see positivity in every situation.

The main process of the day

Today, use the place you are and be thankful for all possibilities behind it.

Today, be free, joyful, thankful, positive and optimistic before, during and after every situation.

Today, use miraculous power of the possibility to be. Be for a while in peace and silence, during which you are focused on quietness of that flowing moment. Just feel that flowing freedom (it's about the awareness of the possibility to be free).

Today's experience?

ay six

Main theme of the day

The power of your five senses – the nose

The five senses are not only physiological senses, they are the primarily ability to immediate receive and influence your current reality.

The nose is a materialized mediator of your ability to receive, transfer and transform the life energy. This is a continual process that happens even when you sleep. Therefore, choose everything carefully and conscientiously.

The main process of the day

Today, focus on the first and the last received situation and describe what it has done with you.

Today, use one situation where you are focused on the ability to receive, transfer and transform the life energy.

Today, use miraculous power of the nose (not the smelling, but the nose). Do any joyful activity in the nature, during which you are focused on all the situations where you can use your nose. Just feel the connection and possibility to use the nose.

Today's experience?

ay seven

Main theme of the day

The power of your five senses – the tongue

(The five senses are not only physiological senses, they are the primarily
ability to immediate receive and influence your current reality.)

The tongue is a materialized mediator of your ability to
receive, transfer and transform the life energy.
Therefore understand, choose, receive and accept only
joyful and peaceful situations (see only the best possibilities in any result).

The main process of the day

*Today, focus on the first and the last accepted situation
and describe what it has done with you.*

*Today, understand, choose, receive and accept one joy-
ful situation, to feel all the beautiful emotions behind
them.*

*Today, use miraculous power of the tongue. Do any joy-
ful activity in the nature, during which you are focused
on all the situations where you can use your tongue (not
the tasting, but the tongue). Just feel the connection and
possibility to use the tongue.*

Today's experience?

ay eight

Main theme of the day

The power of your five senses – the eyes

(The five senses are not only physiological senses, they are the primarily ability to immediate receive and influence your current reality.)

The eyes are a materialized mediator of your ability to receive, transfer and transform the life energy.
Therefore, choose such a kind of using your eyes, which keep them in a relaxing and healthy condition.

The main process of the day

Today, focus on the first and the last using (inside of you or outside of you) of your eyes and describe what it has done with you.

Today, use some eye exercises to feel them relaxed and healthy.

Today, use miraculous power of the eyes. Do any joyful activity in the nature, during which you are focused on all the situations where you can use your eyes (not the seeing, but the eyes). Just feel the connection and possibility to use the eyes.

Today's experience?

ay nine

Main theme of the day

The power of your five senses – the skin

(The five senses are not only physiological senses, they are the primarily ability to immediate receive and influence your current reality.)

The skin is the materialized mediator of your ability to receive, transfer, transform and hold secure the life energy.

Therefore, choose such a kind of using your skin, which keep them in a shining, flexible and healthy condition.

The main process of the day

Today, focus on the first and the last feeling of your skin (not touching, but the whole skin feeling) and describe what it has done with you.

Today, observe your skin how it react on different situations.

Today, use miraculous power of the skin. Do any joyful activity in the nature, during which you are focused on all the situations where you can use your skin (not the touching, but the skin). Just feel the connection and possibility to use the skin.

Today's experience?

ay ten

Main theme of the day

The power of your five senses – the ears

(The five senses are not only physiological senses, they are the primarily ability to immediate receive and influence your current reality.)

The ears are a materialized mediator of your ability to receive, transfer and transform the life energy.
Therefore, choose such a kind of using your ears, which keep them in a peaceful, quiet and healthy condition.

The main process of the day

Today, focus on the first and the last feeling of your ears (not hearing, but the ears feeling that they are) and describe what it has done with you.

Today, observe your ears how they react on different situations.

Today, use miraculous power of the ears. Do any joyful activity in the nature, during which you are focused on all the situations where you can use your ears (not the hearing, but the ears). Just feel the connection and possibility to use the ears.

Today's experience?

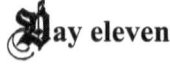 **ay eleven**

Main theme of the day

The power of actions – the purification

The power of actions is not only your physical ability, it is the primarily process to immediate transform your current reality.

The purification process or action is a way of elimination or abandonment all the unpleasant situations.

Therefore, you must be aware of your actions.

The main process of the day

Today, focus on your first and the last action (inside of you or outside of you) and describe what it has done with you.

Today, look back on your most used mechanical actions and make them a conscious process.

Today, use miraculous power of the purification. Do any joyful activity in the nature, during which you are focused on the beautiful possibility of self-purification of the nature. Just feel the connection with this process (it's about the awareness of the possibility to feel the process of purification).

Today's experience?

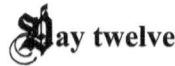ay twelve

Main theme of the day

The power of actions – the reproduction

(The power of actions is not only your physical ability, it is the primarily
process to immediate transform your current reality.)

The reproduction process or action is a way of re-materi-
alizing your all past thoughts, words and actions. It is
your possibility to be and not to be, to materialize or not
to materialize.

Therefore, you must produce and grow in yourselves
only the purest virtues.

The main process of the day

*Today, focus on the four temperaments and describe
which of them is most active in you and how you can harmonize them that they work as one.*

*Today, use some relaxation or meditation techniques to
regenerate your mental and physical condition.*

*Today, use miraculous power of the reproduction. Do
any joyful activity in the nature, during which you are focused on the beautiful possibility of reproduction and regeneration of the nature. Just feel the connection with
this process (it's about the awareness of the possibility to
feel the process of reproduction and regeneration).*

Today's experience?

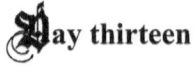 ## ay thirteen

Main theme of the day

The power of actions – the movement

(The power of actions is not only your physical ability, it is the primarily process to immediate transform your current reality.)

The movement process or action is a way how to transfer information values in the current time and space. It is your possibility to be in the right time, at the right place and with the right beings.

Therefore, you must be flexible and healthy, both mentally and physically.

The main process of the day

Today, focus on your first and the last movement (inside of you or outside of you) and describe what it has done with you.

Today, use some stretching techniques to make your mental and physical condition be in the joyfully state.

Today, use miraculous power of the movement. Do any joyful activity in the nature, during which you are focused on all the beautiful possibility of movement. Just feel the connection with this process (it's about the awareness of the possibility to feel the process of movement).

Today's experience?

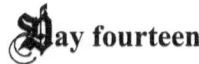ay fourteen

Main theme of the day

The power of actions – the grasping and holding

(The power of actions is not only your physical ability, it is the primarily process to immediate transform your current reality.)

The grasping and holding process or action is a way how to receive and own the best information values. It is your possibility to be what you want to be, to have what you want to have and to handle with everything already acquired how you want.

Therefore, you must use only peaceful and harmonious gestures.

The main process of the day

Today, focus on your first and the last hands movement (inside of you or outside of you) and describe what it has done with you.

Today, use only peaceful and harmonious gestures and observe what it has done with you and others.

Today, use miraculous power of the hands movement. Do any joyful activity in the nature, during which you are focused on all the beautiful possibility of hands movement. Just feel the connection with this process (it's about the awareness of the possibility to feel the process of hands movement).

Today's experience?

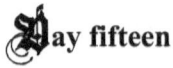

Day fifteen

Main theme of the day

The power of actions – the speech

(The power of actions is not only your physical ability, it is the primarily process to immediate transform your current reality.)

The speech process or action is a way how to transform the current time and space in the meaning to make an information value present, relative or real. It is your possibility to change all manifestations and materializations. Therefore, you must use only peaceful thoughts, words and actions.

The main process of the day

Today, focus on your first and the last word (inside of you or outside of you) and describe what it has done with you.

Today, use only peaceful and harmonious words and observe what it has done with you and others.

Today, use miraculous power of the words. Do any joyful activity in the nature, during which you are focused on all the beautiful possibility of speaking and to be quiet. Just feel the connection with this process (it's about the awareness of the possibility to feel the process of choosing between speaking or to be quiet).

Today's experience?

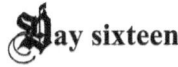ay sixteen

Main theme of the day

The power of your five sensations – the smelling

The five sensations are not only physiological senses, they are the primarily ability to immediate receive and influence your current reality.

The sensation of smelling exceeds your thinking mind and brings you to the harmonious state. Therefore, choose consciously fragrances around you. It is a way to learn knowingly and willingly to receive and influence everything you really wish for.

The main process of the day

Today, focus on the first and the last fragrance you smelled and describe what it has done with you.

Today, use your favorite fragrance, to feel the ability that you can receive and influence everything you wish for.

Today, use miraculous power of the smell. Do any joyful activity in the nature, during which you are focused on all the fragrances around you. Just feel the connection and possibility to smell (it's about the awareness of the possibility to feel the smelling process).

Today's experience?

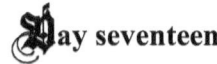

ay seventeen

Main theme of the day

The power of your five sensations – the tasting

(The five sensations are not only physiological senses, they are the primarily
ability to immediate receive and influence your current reality.)

The sensation of tasting refers to all the different feelings
and experiences of your daily life. Therefore, choose
such a kind of activity that is more an art than necessity
and which relates to aesthetics that create beautiful emotions for all beings.

The main process of the day

*Today, focus on the first and the last taste you received
and describe what it has done with you.*

*Today, use your favorite food and do what you enjoy
most, to feel all the beautiful emotions behind them.*

*Today, use miraculous power of the taste. Do any joyful
activity in the nature, during which you are focused on
all the beauty you can taste everywhere around you. Just
feel the connection and possibility to taste (it's about the
awareness of the possibility to feel the process of experiencing).*

Today's experience?

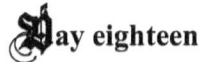ay eighteen

Main theme of the day

The power of your five sensations – the seeing

(The five sensations are not only physiological senses, they are the primarily ability to immediate receive and influence your current reality.)

The sensation of seeing is affected by using three concepts. These concepts are "physical / non-physical" forms, "visible / invisible" forms and "named / nameless" form. Therefore, choose such a kind of form or objects you are looking at, which brings you freedom and joy.

The main process of the day

Today, focus on the first and the last seen form or object (inside of you or outside of you) and describe what it has done with you.

Today, use your favorite form or object and observe it to feel all the beautiful emotions behind them.

Today, use miraculous power of the seeing. Do any joyful activity in the nature, during which you are focused on the beautiful forms or objects around you. Just feel the connection and possibility to see (it's about the awareness of the possibility to feel the process of vision).

Today's experience?

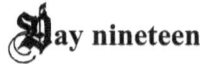**ay nineteen**

Main theme of the day

The power of your five sensations – the touching

(The five sensations are not only physiological senses, they are the primarily ability to immediate receive and influence your current reality.)

The sensation of touching is affected by using three concepts. These concepts are "object / non-object" forms, "sensation of the object / non-object" forms and "knowing of the object / non-object" form. Therefore, choose such a kind of form or objects you are touching, which brings you absolutely satisfaction.

The main process of the day

Today, focus on the first and the last touched form or object (inside of you or outside of you) and describe what it has done with you.

Today, use your favorite form or object and feel all the beautiful emotions behind touching (mental of physical) them.

Today, use miraculous power of the touching. Do any joyful activity in the nature, during which you are focused on the beautiful forms or objects around you. Just feel the connection and possibility to touch (it's about the awareness of the possibility to feel the process of touching).

Today's experience?

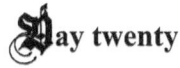

Day twenty

Main theme of the day

The power of your five sensations – the hearing

(The five sensations are not only physiological senses, they are the primarily
ability to immediate receive and influence your current reality.)

The sensation of hearing is a way of acquiring knowledge. Hearing is the ability to receive all of information values (internal or unmanifested as well as external or manifested) at once and transform them according to your current needs.

Therefore, search only conversations that enrich you.

The main process of the day

Today, focus on the first and the last heard sound (inside of you or outside of you) and describe what it has done with you.

Today, use your favorite sound and feel all the beautiful emotions behind listening (mental of physical) them.

Today, use miraculous power of your hearing. Do any joyful activity in the nature, during which you are focused on the beautiful sounds around you. Just feel the connection and possibility to hear (it's about the awareness of the possibility to feel the process of hearing).

Today's experience?

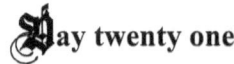ay twenty one

Main theme of the day

The power of your body

Your body is the materialized matter of your past thoughts, words and actions. It is a vehicle of health and healing. Health is an indicator that everything in your entire life is perfect or in harmony - as it should be, as your nature is. Healing is your ability to transform something unpleasant or in relative state to something beautiful. Therefore, learn by knowing your inner world, how to properly care for your materialized body or holly temple and strengthen your full potential.

The main process of the day

Today, focus on the first and the last feeling of your body and describe what it has done with you.

Today, use some relaxing or meditative techniques, to feel the beauty of your whole body.

Today, use miraculous power of your body. Do any joyful activity in the nature, during which you are focused on all the situations where you can use your whole body. Just feel the connection and possibility to be in the physical body.

Today's experience?

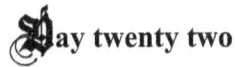ay twenty two

Main theme of the day

The power of creation principles – capacity for thought

The capacity for thought is regulated by your will, through your body, through and speeches, all as a multi-dimensional communication system. This capacity or better to say capacity materialization space has no limitations and is infinitely expandable and manipulable (transformable).

Therefore, use your full potential to fill it in the right way.

The main process of the day

Today, focus on the capacity of the elements (earth, water, air, fire and aether (aether is not a space) and describe what it has done with you.

Today, use some relaxing or meditative techniques, to feel the beauty of your thoughts and how they filled your daily life.

Today, use miraculous power of capacity. Do any joyful activity in the nature, during which you are focused on the limitlessness of the whole universe. Just feel the connection and possibility to have limitless capacity of everything.

Today's experience?

# Day twenty three

Main theme of the day

The power of creation principles – separation concept

The separation concept is a protective system that helping you by manifestations and materializations of specific products of your thoughts, words and actions. It is not always negative, it is just a possibility how to present your current personality patterns, which can be described also as the multiplicated ego (ego is the sum of all your individual behavioral and other properties).

Therefore, use your individual behavioral and other properties in the name of freedom a joy.

The main process of the day

Today, focus for a moment on the separation process itself and describe what it has done with you.

Negative separation works by separating of willpower and desire, with using more desire. Use them today as a unity.

Today, use miraculous power of separation. Do any joyful activity in the nature, during which you are focused on the fascinating process of separation in the nature. Just feel the connection and possibility to separate.

Today's experience?

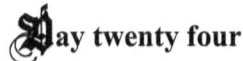ay twenty four

Main theme of the day

The power of creation principles – reason

The concept of reason you can achieve only by your intuition. This reason has nothing to do with a social limited reason, this reason is combination of willpower and all your information values at once, this is the place of all your power.

Therefore, use the great joy to find the most amazing and best-felt situations and people you wish for.

The main process of the day

Today, use the great joy by finding some situation or person you wish for and describe what it has done with you.

Today, perform only gentle and peaceful activities (thoughts, words, actions - mental and physical), use relaxing, meditation, or other techniques to help you achieve a refinement of your body and everything during the day.

Today, use miraculous power of reason. Do any joyful activity in the nature, during which you let your intuition emerge. Just feel the connection and possibility to intuitive see the reason.

Today's experience?

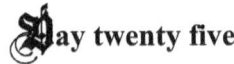 ## Day twenty five

Main theme of the day

The power of creation – the primal created matter

The concept of primal created matter is based in your ability to group, separate and harmonize. The conscious harmonization of grouping and separating (all the modifications of your whole "to be") is the primal created matter of form or object or situation and so on.

Don't forget, your mind is the subtlest aspect of your multidimensionality and your body is the most tangible manifestation and materialization of your mind. Therefore, use your mind and body as one concept.

The main process of the day

Today, choose one situation where you will act with awareness of the connection of mind and body and describe what it has done with you.

Today, choose one situation that you harmonize by separating and grouping.

Today, use miraculous power of productivity. Do any joyful activity in the nature, during which you are focused on the productivity of everything around you. Just feel the connection and possibility to be part of that wonderful productivity.

Today's experience?

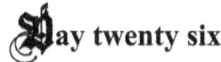 ay twenty six

Main theme of the day

The power of creation – the consciousness

The concept of your whole "to be" is ruled by the power of consciousness, which is the summarization of the principles of nature. It is the form of the absolute consciousness, it is the emboided field of knowing. Your consciousness is a beautiful uncaused principle. Therefore, you must know the consciousness, use the consciousness and be the consciousness.

The main process of the day

Today, focus on the first and the last moment with realization of unity and describe what it has done with you.

Today, choose one handwork (such as jigsaw puzzle) in which you can summarize all components.

Today, use miraculous power of consciousness. Do any joyful activity in the nature, during which you are focused on the immensity of unity around you. Just feel the connection and possibility to be one with universe.

Today's experience?

 **ay twenty seven**

Main theme of the day

The power of concept behind – the causality

The concept of causality binds you with all your daily situations, both pleasant and unpleasant. The causality is your current time, place and proximity (with other beings, situations, etc.). It is a mighty confirmation by materializing your thoughts.

Therefore, you must perform actions (thoughts, words and actions as one) unattached to the relativity of some final outcome (for example, not attributing importance).

The main process of the day

Today, focus on the first and the last moment without realization of importance and describe what it has done with you.

Today, use only the concept of freedom. Just be free from the concept of importance.

Today, use miraculous power of causality. Do any joyful activity in the nature, during which you are focused on how the all existing objects around you pass through cycles. Just feel the connection and possibility to observe it.

Today's experience?

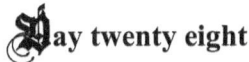

Day twenty eight

Main theme of the day

The power of concept behind – the time

The concept of time is nourished by your awareness of
the past and future (egocentric desires, hopeful expectations, worry, anger and anxiety, etc.). This 40 day system
and also no other system in the universe force you to act
in the sense of time and space. They are indicators of
how you can bring everything into unity and live or be in
well-being without "awareness of..."

Therefore, see the things or situation or universe or life
itself as they really are.

The main process of the day

*Today, focus on the first and the last moment without
awareness of to be and describe what it has done with
you.*

*Today, just be peace and quiet in every situation, both
mental and physical.*

*Today, use miraculous power behind time. Do any joyful
activity in the nature, during which you are focused on
how the all existing objects around you pass through
time. Just feel the connection and possibility to flow
through that observing experience.*

Today's experience?

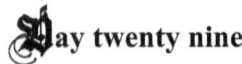 **ay twenty nine**

Main theme of the day

The power of concept behind – the desire

The concept of desire is a separation from reality. Everything you've been up to this moment was just a materialization of your past desires separated from reality. You thought you needed something (non-specific) to have something another (less-specific). Therefore, when you gets any other desire fulfilled, you found that you were still unsatisfied.

Therefore, you must use the willpower with desire together as one concept for creating.

The main process of the day

Today, choose one situation in which you use the "secret" power of effort to be free from desire and describe what it has done with you.

Today, use gratitude for the possibility to know about the "secret" power of effort.

Today, use miraculous power behind desire. Do any joyful activity in the nature, during which you are free from any desire. Just feel the connection and possibility to be and observe the nature without any expectations.

Today's experience?

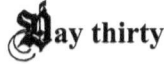ay thirty

Main theme of the day

The power of concept behind – the incompleteness

The concept of incompleteness is ruled by believes which we ca describe as a statement "I think it can be". This is not ignorance, it is only an insufficiently grouped or materialized concept of knowledge, for example expressed by your presence (by your statements). It is only a part of knowledge itself.

Therefore, as I have mentioned several times, you must know and not to think that you know.

The main process of the day

Today, use incompleteness as a premise of completeness and describe what it has done with you.

Today, be free from all believes and enjoy the things as they are.

Today, use miraculous power behind incompleteness. Do any joyful activity in the nature, during which you are focused on the perfection of everything around you. Just feel the connection and possibility to be part of this perfection.

Today's experience?

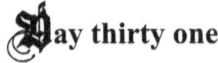

Day thirty one

Main theme of the day

The power of concept behind – the art

The concept of art is customizable in any way. It is a space that contains all the possibilities (the entire universe at once) in a potential state and which, on the basis of your most overriding requirements, manifests itself. It is a standard algorithmic process with the task entry "find - connect - materialize". This algorithm is created by yourself (unless you allow it by putting yourself into the slave role).

Therefore, design your way you live only by yourself.

The main process of the day

Today, use your first and the last action as a beautiful art of living and describe what it has done with you.

Today, choose one simple situation which you can handle and do it. Describe what has changed due to finalizing of this process?

Today, use miraculous power behind the art. Do any joyful activity in the nature, during which you are focused on the constantly changing processes around you. Just feel the connection and possibility to be able handle it.

Today's experience?

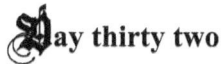

Day thirty two

Main theme of the day

The power of inner concept – the harmony

The concept of harmony is in the knowledge that you are a materialized unity. This knowledge must be confirmed by the right thoughts, words and actions. You have to realize, that the right thoughts, words, actions, goals and results are all one. There is no difference, there is only knowing.

Therefore, be "open" to feelings of interconnection with all beings, with the whole universe and with everything you know as also which you don't know.

The main process of the day

Today, use your first and the last action as a one concept and describe what it has done with you.

Today, choose one simple situation in which you are using your consciousness, that there is absolute balance between "I" and "This".

Today, use miraculous power behind the harmony. Do any joyful activity in the nature, during which you are focused on the sonic and other forms around you. Just feel the connection and possibility to knowing them.

Today's experience?

Day thirty three

Main theme of the day

The power of inner concept – the mastering

The concept of mastering is supported by freedom. Freedom is the universal principle of your life. There is only one single question, "Are you ready for freedom or not?" Therefore, you must be free from all sufferings, duality concepts and social desires.

The main process of the day

Today, use your first and the last thought, word and action with gratitude for possibility to used them and describe what it has done with you.

Today, choose one simple situation in which you feel absolutely free and answer that question "Are you ready for freedom or not?"

Today, use miraculous power behind the freedom. Do any joyful activity in the nature, during which you are enjoying the absolutely freedom around you. Just feel the connection and possibility to be free.

Today's experience?

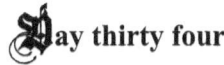

Day thirty four

Main theme of the day

The power of inner concept – the willpower

The concept of willpower is the first imaginary movement into differentiation. Through the power of will, through this particular place or space or algorithm in yourself, you are capable materialize everything. Therefore, you must be always free, joyful and satisfied with everything, because even a suffering person can easily find freedom and happiness from deep within.

The main process of the day

Today, use your first and the last thought, word and action with gratitude for possibility to used them and describe what it has done with you.

Today, choose one simple situation in which you use your willpower to achieve the wanted and desired result without thinking, talking and acting about it.

Today, use miraculous power behind the willpower. Do any joyful activity in the nature, during which you enjoy the creative willpower which are created everything around you. Just feel the connection and possibility to use the will.

Today's experience?

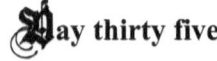

Day thirty five

Main theme of the day

The transformative power

The concept of transformative power is energy itself. It is the specific energy which allows you to view your powers more as expressions of the whole universe rather than the social generated egos.

Therefore, you must be aware of you're the power inside of you.

The main process of the day

Today, use your first and the last thought, word and action as a transformative power and describe what it has done with you.

Today, choose one simple situation which you transform into something different (change the already finished status to something "new" – for example drinking coffee to tea drinking, reading messages on your phone to read the book and so on).

Today, use miraculousness behind the transformative power. Do any joyful activity in the nature, during which you enjoy the flowing transformational power around you. Just feel the connection and possibility to be able, to do.

Today's experience?

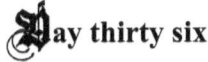

ay thirty six

Main theme of the day

The aspect of multiple paradoxes

The concept of multiple paradoxes is, that not everything that appeared to you to be unpleasant should result in harming you. It's a way of real regeneration, regardless of your social feelings. In this space of multiple paradoxes lies the cause of all creation and the establishment of order with the ending of the unnecessary.

Therefore, you must be strong during each life situation.

The main process of the day

Today, use your first and the last thought, word and action in order to see the multiple paradoxes behind them and describe what it has done with you.

Today, choose one simple situation in which you use unorthodox, non-standard and unexpected process.

Today, use miraculous power behind the multiple paradoxes. Do any joyful activity in the nature, during which you enjoy the flowing paradoxes around you. Just feel the connection and possibility to be and not to be at the same time.

Today's experience?

Day thirty seven

Main theme of the day

The aspect of the perfect multiple unity

The concept of perfect multiple unity is hidden in the wisdom of all beginnings and endings of everything. This concept has many levels of meaning and application. In this state you are empowered and blessed (without fear, worry anxiety and depression) and more compassionate, which evokes in you the peace and increases mental and physical health.

Therefore, you must be free from all social systems, from your own beliefs and from everything at all. Not to be separated, just to be free.

The main process of the day

Today, use the first and the last moment of 10 simple situations in order to see the multiple unity behind them and describe what it has done with you.

Today, choose only love in your expressions.

Today, use miraculous power behind the multiple unity. Do any joyful activity in the nature, during which you are enjoyed the beginnings, endings and unity around you. Just feel the connection and possibility to love.

Today's experience?

Day thirty eight

Main theme of the day

The aspect of absolute creation

The concept of absolute creation is supported by the right decisions in the right way. It is the truth and fearlessness itself. Without practicing truth and fearlessness you cannot achieve and use this state and aspect. It is beyond everything and it is also beyond the concept of beyond. Therefore, you must be outside, beyond, before, after, etc., simply be absolutely beyond all descriptions and beyond everything you cannot describe.

The main process of the day

Today, be fearless in all situations and describe what it has done with you.

Today, choose only truth in your expressions.

Today, use miraculous power behind the possibility to be beyond. Do any joyful activity in the nature, during which you are enjoyed the absoluteness around you. Just feel the connection and possibility to be fearless.

Today's experience?

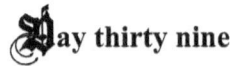

ay thirty nine

Main theme of the day

The causa causarum

The causa causarum is indescribable in our languages,
but is absolutely experienceable. You have perfect inner
possibility to experience everything you need. That's
great to know and that's why you are so unique.

You are, so you can!

Therefore, you must be aware of your all possibilities and
help the others (when they are ready for help) in order for
them to exchange the two words "good" and "evil" for
peace and silence.

The main process of the day

*Today, take advantage of the opportunity not to act and
describe what it has done with you.*

Today, choose only peace and silence.

*Today, use miraculous power behind the causa
causarum. That requires your non-action in action and
action in non-action, therefore choose all the knowing of
universe to practice it. Search in nature, search in universe, search in yourself.*

Today's experience?

# Day forty

Main theme of the day

The success

The success is final synthesis, the success is you. You have inside of you all the possibilities to rebuild everything. This rebuilding process means successfulness. Successfulness is returning you before the beginning of creation. It's a wonderful way to imagine an imaginary circle of creation.

Therefore, you have love yourself and everything and you have to be thankful to everyone and for everything.

The main process of the day

Today, concentrate on your waking up and falling asleep as a bliss of successfulness and describe what it has done with you.

Today, see successfulness in all beings and situations.

Today, use miraculous power behind the success. Do any joyful activity in the nature, during which you are enjoyed the successfulness around you. Just feel the connection and possibility to be successful.

Today's experience?

Bonus chapter two

"The machinery of multidimensional business space is transformable by your energy system."

MACHINERY OF BUSINESS

𝕿here is another one big question in the process of succeeding which I often hear. This question was:

"What to use to be interesting for the whole market? Is there anything that can fascinate or dominate the entire market without exception?"

Your one and only job in a business machinery is to offer a functional process that will bring your clients and customers into a state of success. Therefore, stop shaming, forcing and extorting others with some fake slogans as "Are you ready to make the biggest step in your career? If you miss our program, it will be hard for you to achieve it.", or other similar psycho-marketing manipulations. You must be just honest and true.

The functional process that will bring your clients and customers into a state of success is focusing on them as on success itself. Just as you already know, you are the success itself, you have to accept that they are also the success itself. It's up to you to show them the right way to understand and practice it.

irst step

You have to know that you are the success.

econd step

You have to know the freedom and beauty of your uniqueness.

hird step

You have to absolutely thrust in everything you do and offer.

Fourth step

You have to know the value of what you offer.

Fifth step

You have to know what benefit it has for others.

Sixth step

You have to know the right way for everyone. You are not changing others, you are showing others all the opportunities to be a success itself.

eventh step

Your change is a change for others.

Next logical step is the successfulness that leads to success itself. "Leading to" means that your clients and customers must be in the connection with beauty the energy currency of money or successfulness. This energy currency is abundance.

We are grateful and we love the abundance of peace and silence.
We are grateful and we love the abundance of the universe.
We are grateful and we love the abundance of life.
We are grateful and we love the abundance of knowing.
We are grateful and we love the abundance of sleep.
We are grateful and we love the abundance of awakening.
We are grateful and we love the abundance to breathe.
We are grateful and we love the abundance of freedom.
We are grateful and we love the abundance of joy.
We are grateful and we love the abundance of our thoughts, words and actions.
Our thought create, manifest and materialize constant wealth, prosperity and abundance.
Our speech create, manifest and materialize constant wealth, prosperity and abundance.
Our actions create, manifest and materialize constant wealth, prosperity and abundance.
We are grateful and we love the abundance of everything materialized.
We are grateful and we love the abundance of creation.
We are grateful and we love the abundance of nature.
We are grateful and we love the abundance itself.

Your clients and customers must understand the power of communication and what's more, they must know if they are really ready to be success itself. To help your clients and customers know if they are really ready to be success itself, you can help them with the following practices about which I first wrote for you a few very important information. These practices can be used as short-term (1 - 12 days), but also as a long-term process (12 days plus). Everything depends on the current requirement, but you have to know, that it is the creation of freedom for oneself for "new and better" creation – the regeneration of whole system. It is a mastering of one skill, but in the same time is it the improvement of all other skills. This is a continuous process that makes you, your clients and your customers become conscious creators of the demand.

There are three primary levels before this practices:

1. **Ethics** – of behavior, thinking, speaking and actions. This is achieved exactly by *"the activities management process in relation to themselves"*. Just stop be negative at all, stop all that relativity of suffering.
2. **Pay more attention to others** – is the next logical step, because if one (you, your clients or your customers) is working on removing negatives, he becomes successful more and more and have no more so big need to own. He is so called "cultivated businessman".
3. **100% attention on others** – is the final purpose to master the whole machinery of business.

Let's go to the practices mentioned above:

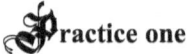ractice one

"You don't need to tolerate anything you disagree with."

Before falling asleep and by waking up, have the intention to be intuitive and find something you really want.

Three times a day meditate on your intent.

All day, observe only what you really want.

Be patient.

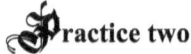ractice two

"You are able to do the best for yourself and others."

Trust absolutely in your possibilities and abilities.

Recognize that everywhere is everything enough for everyone.

All day, be thankful for wealth, prosperity and abundance around you.

Be joyful.

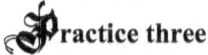ractice three

The third practice consists only of freedom.
Just create and receive fruits of your amazingness.

The machinery of business has amazing information faces. You can use all of them. By choosing and practicing them you reconstructing the whole mindset of yourself, your clients and customers. Therefore, you must be oriented in this infinite variations of multidimensional information values. Everyone is part of the abundance, that's the fact. The general meaning of the business machinery is that one needs the others to be successful or in other words, to be fully realized. This idea has a dual meaning. Either you play a central role in the business or you need someone else to be successful in the business. Either you are the one with whom others want to be and are connected or you need to be and are connected with others. It is undeniable that you need to use common experience. Liberation is my favorite experience and therefore I invite you to experience it.

It is said that liberation is possible only by the absolute destruction of negativity. But you already know that duality is only a concept of neverending possibilities how to achieve harmonization. So what negativity destruction we should talk about? Liberation is the harmonious state of abundance (the perfect combination of everything) that provides successfulness in all areas of your life. Liberation is the last piece of puzzle to understand that success is you. It is the most passive principle of all principles and therefore it seemed for many people that successfulness was very slow and difficult to achieve. Passivity of liberation is also an enormous reception activity. The honest reception is the answer to your liberation. Receive with love and knowledge, receive wisely and deliberately, receive with joy and happiness. Liberation have its own structure:

- credibility, resilience and collaboration, which builds and raise a healthier business process;
- sincerity, sacrifice and tolerance with sincerity and discretion, which builds and raise the absolute competence of the offered business;
- communication, empathy, compassion, the ability to listen and the ability to help, which builds and raise the business popularity;
- responsibility, which builds and raise all the business possibilities;

You have to use compassion, generosity, kindness, determination, optimism, satisfaction, joy, joyful and peaceful activity, loyalty, honesty, generosity, sacrifice, devotion, motivation and never betray or cheat the others out of personal, social or any other interest. Also, stop making problems worse than they were. For example, if you have seen anger or whatever you considered as a negative situation, do not give value to it. Don't overpowering it, it is away and it no longer can hurt anyone. Take your attention away from it and observe something beautiful. This is way of liberation. In other words, you have to go beyond what you observed to see what you have not seen in yourselves. You must see everything in a "new and better" way – see everything as it really is.

I have good news for you. By application of the attention you are liberated. By changing how you pay attention, you immediately change what you are experiencing. At the same moment you change also what your business is and of course who you are.

Are there any support steps of liberation? Yes, they are! They are part of the whole process of business machinery. Use them in the best way:

1. Understanding

This is done systematically in the process of your meditation and relaxation practices. Use following steps:

- Observe your thoughts, words and actions
- Observe the system of world
- Observe the system of universe
- Let the situations flow as they are

2. Coordinating

This is done automatically after practicing of your meditation and relaxation practices. Use following steps:

- Combine your thoughts, words and actions in only one direction
- Combine your thoughts, words and actions with the system of world you observe
- Combine your thoughts, words and actions with the system of universe you observe
- Let the situations appear as a concept for transforming

3. Experience

This is done automatically after coordination process in your daily life as a logical result. Use following steps:

- Let the experience be the experience without assigning importance
- Use gratitude
- Confirm the experience with conscious understanding

Example one – money multiplying:

- Observe your thoughts, words and actions
- Combine your thoughts, words and actions in only one direction
- Let the situations flow as they are
- Let the situations appear as a concept for transforming
- Let the experience be the experience without assigning importance
- Use gratitude
- Confirm the experience with conscious understanding

If you **observe** your thoughts, words and actions and **combine** them with the *money multiplying*, by **letting the situations flow** as they are, you get the exact concept prepared for the **transformation** in your meditation or relaxation technique.

Now, **transform** the exact concept of the *money multiplying* in current time and space as if had already happened.

By doing this, you've activated a system that brought you in your daily life a concrete experience connected with this process.

Now, *let the experience be* the experience without assigning importance to the *money multiplying* and use **gratitude** for the possibility to experience it. **Confirmation** is a conscious knowledge of this whole process.

The result of this process was (by my friends and clients):
- the experience of liberation;
- the experience of money multiplying in daily life;
- the experience of satisfaction;

Example two – finding the right product for sale:
- Observe the system of world
- Combine your thoughts, words and actions with the system of world you observe
- Let the situations flow as they are
- Let the situations appear as a concept for transforming
- Let the experience be the experience without assigning importance
- Use gratitude
- Confirm the experience with conscious understanding

If you **observe** the system of world and **combine** them with the *finding the right product for sale*, by **letting the situations flow** as they are, you get the exact concept prepared for the **transformation** in your meditation or relaxation technique.

Now, **transform** the exact concept of the *finding the right product for sale* in current time and space as if it had already happened.

By doing this, you've activated a system that brought you in your daily life a concrete experience connected with this process.

Now, **let the experience be** the experience without assigning importance to the *finding the right product for sale* and use **gratitude** for the possibility to experience it. **Confirmation** is a conscious knowledge of this whole process.

The result of this process was (by my friends and clients):

- the experience of liberation;
- the experience of finding the right product for sale in the business strategy;
- the experience of satisfaction;

Example three – finding the abundance:

- Observe the system of universe
- Combine your thoughts, words and actions with the system of universe you observe
- Let the situations flow as they are
- Let the situations appear as a concept for transforming
- Let the experience be the experience without assigning importance
- Use gratitude
- Confirm the experience with conscious understanding

If you **observe** the system of universe and **combine** them with the *finding the abundance*, by **letting the situations** *flow* as they are, you get the exact concept prepared for the **transformation** in your meditation or relaxation technique.

Now, **transform** the exact concept of the *finding the abundance* in current time and space as if the abundance flow through you.

By doing this, you've activated a system that brought you in your daily life a concrete experience connected with this process.

Now, *let the experience be* the experience without assigning importance to the *finding the abundance* and use **gratitude** for the possibility to experience it. **Confirmation** is a conscious knowledge of this whole process.

The result of this process was (by my friends and clients):

- the experience of liberation;
- the experience of understanding what the abundance is;
- the experience of satisfaction;

These demonstrations or examples shows you how to combine obviously uncombinable options. This is a system of synchronicity and it is also a game with your daily routine. Understanding, coordinating and experiencing are wonderful support steps of liberation. The materialization of liberation converts you into citizens of business machinery. Therefore, always act simply and harmoniously, because the results are amazing!

The machinery of the multidimensional business space is absolute freely programmable, customizable, transformable and any time materializable by your own energy system. Just choose the right tool, in the right time, at the right place and towards the right beings and situations.

Liberation is an imaginary abundance point in the multidimensional business space. There is a concrete space of your multidimensionality in which all your experiences unite into a concrete knowable point from which all your materializations arose. The liberation is possible to describe as a relative near beginning and ending of the finest aspect of your beautiful mind. It is beyond the time, space and causation and is the possibility to your absolute potential.

By understanding the liberation point of these practices or possibilities, all of the other practices can be done in absolutely ease. These information values on this perspective are for you all who was able and ready to ask – to read this book. You wanted to see the big answer of success with a clear vision of the possible way and the tools of attaining your greatest goal. The greatest goal is you and therefore the whole machinery of business belongs you.

"May the wealth, prosperity and abundance constantly flow through you, that you can spread it in the right time, at the right place and to the right beings."

CONCLUSION

Beloved friends in knowing, I am addressing you all the miraculous and successful greetings. On these 333 pages, I have presented you one opportunity to be where you want to be, whatever you want to be, to have everything you want to have and to know that you are the success itself.

When you made the experience that the success is you, your experiences are more than symbolic successfulness. You have achieved powerful predispositions inside of you, which is the ultimate premise for all your wanted and desired successful materializations.

When you think, speak and act in the right way, you feel free, joyful and satisfied. You attract goodness, you create goodness inside and around you and you enjoy all the wonderful fruits of your success. Many want the results right away, like in a sci-fi movie. Only because they did not see the results right away doesn't mean nothing's happening. It also does not mean that they have failed or that they are doing wrong. Definitely not. Everything you do, you do it the best way you know at the current moment. You all are great as you are. Everybody must know it. Already before the moment of unmanifested communication, all the necessary means and possibilities are created and ready to materialize to all requirements. But you already know it, which is also the liberating step of liberation itself.

Your thoughts, words and actions have miraculous power because they are a connectors between unmanifested and manifested. Therefore, use them wisely, in favor of yourselves and all beings. The following statements may be helpful to you.

We are grateful for all the beautiful knowledge.
Let the manifested knowledge is by all our steps.
Let us be constantly filled with the beauty of knowledge.
Knowledge is a vehicle of creation and we are the peaceful path on which it is still moving.
We are the source of these powerful thoughts, words and actions.
We are the source of wealth, prosperity and abundance.
We are the source of all creations and materializations.
We are the time and place to meet with wealth, prosperity and abundance.
Wherever we are present with our thoughts, words and actions, there are also present the wealth, prosperity and abundance.
Wherever we are present with our thoughts, words and actions, there are also present the peace, silence and harmony.
During these powerful and wonderful thoughts, words and actions that we can express, the beauty of joyfulness materializes everywhere.
Let the miraculous beauty of wealth, prosperity and abundance shine for all beings.

Be inspired by the wisdom that dwells in you and express it in the form of pearls of wisdom for all beings. You have everything you need to permanent reach the well-being. Use your uniqueness and amazingness, because you are unique and amazing. Just be aware of this and believe in the importance of being here to enrich yourself, all beings, the whole world and the universe. You are a valuable part of the eternity that needs your attention.

I am grateful for thoughts, words and actions, for the time and space and for the way you have devoted to this book.

"Now you know the place of creating, now you know that the success is you, now you are the conscious creator, now is the right time and the right place to enjoy your successfulness."

References

"Thank you."

Idries Shah. *Fatima, the Spinner and the Tent (Teaching Story),* March 1, 2006

My personal conversations with my brother Bc. Miroslav Schlesinger

My personal conversations with MUDr. Teodor Rosinský, CSc.

My personal conversations with Viliam Horváth (†2017)

My personal conversations with PhDr. Mgr. D. A. T. Dušan Belko PhD.

My personal conversations with Guru